A FEATHER FROM THE WORLD'S WING

MESSALINA

VESTIGIA

BY
ALGERNON SYDNEY LOGAN

Collected Edition

NATIONAL PUBLISHING COMPANY
PHILADELPHIA
1934

Printed in U. S. A.

A FEATHER
From the World's Wing

A MODERN ROMANCE

PREFACE.

HE who should see in the present book a passionate appeal in favor of any particular opinion or set of opinions would not read it aright. The time for passionate appeals has passed away. Their clang has become unpleasant to our sensitive ears.

Modern machinery is much more noiseless than that in use fifty years ago. The same is true of the machinery of the modern mind. Our intellectual mills are grinding up old beliefs, opinions, customs, with a speed which few of us would wish to accelerate; but there is neither clash nor jar. Many even fairly cultivated people scarcely perceive the process.

To preach in verse against tyranny, though more pardonable, is fully as inartistic as to preach in favor of it; and the following composition would attempt, no matter how feebly, to be a work of art, and not an emancipatory sermon. The province of Art is portrayal rather than discussion, and my endeavor has been to portray a phase of our modern existence which, I believe, has not been hitherto intentionally depicted. This I would call—and the name seems not unapt—the absolute phase. The germs of it are, I believe, in most young persons, taking the form of vague aspirations, which the necessities of life soon

7

dissipate. Almost all of us, however, have known some youth (for extreme youth is the first necessity) in whom the mental state I would call the absolute had attained a seemingly unnatural development. It is this typical condition I have sought to describe. To me it seems one of the most interesting stages of human life; since, when considered in the gross, it is the lash of the steeds of Progress, of which our later and wiser phases are the reins.

In examining this epoch we find much to attract and much to repel us; for, as it is the formative stage, and as the laws which apply to matter apply to mind, we find in this chaotic, inchoate period attraction and repulsion the chief forces. And attraction and repulsion are not merely impressions created in our own minds by the contemplation of this elemental phase: they have their rise and being in the state of mind of which we are speaking, and act outward upon all things around. What we feel is merely the rebound.

If I have, in any sort, succeeded in delineating this absolute phase of life, with its plethora of self-sufficiency and its lack of self-confidence, with its selfishness and its devotion, its ignorance and wisdom, its absurdity and sublimity, I am satisfied.

It may, perhaps justly, be said that the long-winded monologues are inartistic; but it should be remembered that the period I am attempting to draw is not an artistic period, and that to portray it artistically would be inartistic. I believe the egotistical monologue to be a very important symptom of the absolute phase.

The question as to the moral tendency of such accurate sketching is the old one which divides the

two schools of *Art for art* and *Art for morals*. My
dictum would not decide it; so that it seems only
necessary to remind the reader that if all the young
Edmonds in the world were turned loose at once
upon society, with full power to force all their crude
ideas into practice, they would doubtless make more
or less havoc; but that in actual life society is let
loose upon them, and succeeds in taming them without the smallest inconvenience to itself, sometimes,
indeed, making of them the chiefest of its ornaments.

Those who regard a romance with a palpable moral
as little better than a geometrically painted picture,
will not here feel the want of a moral of obtrusive
shape and hue; but there are still many art-loving
persons to whom a good, plain, measurable moral is
not ungrateful. These may, perhaps, find in the catas-
trophe a sufficient reminder of the danger attendant
upon quitting well-trodden paths, and, indeed, the
question,

> "Is it not better, then, to be alone,
> And love Earth only for its earthly sake?"

is one to which one may well hesitate before giving
a reply.

A. S. L.

PHILADELPHIA, June 3, 1885.

A FEATHER
FROM THE WORLD'S WING

CANTO I.

I.

WHAT boots it where these scenes are laid?
  Suffice it that there are such scenes.
Why mark the very spot, the blade
  Of grass on which the fancy leans?
One common country owns us all,
Where'er the Western sunbeams fall.

The land beneath whose new-turned soil
  The future, like the locust, sleeps.
Near by, she, mountain-like, doth foil
  The eye by wild unsightly steeps—
But cross the ocean, would you see
The whole in its sublimity.

Who calls her to the coming race?
  Columbia looks across the sea,
And meets Brittania's thoughtful face;
  But green traditions creepingly
Have round her lovely limbs entwined,
So close they every movement bind.

Mother of freedom, France! thy child
  Roams homeless still, though thou dost keep
His image in thy bosom wild—
  I love thee, and with thee I weep,
Beholding the dull weight of care
Thy hapless citizen must bear:

Weighed down by weapons, that he may
  Confront his watchful enemy;
From books and musings torn away,
  To learn the trade to make men die;
Oppressed by prying legislation,
The bane of every age and nation.

Still farther on, a darker scene—
  Behold a helmet broad and strong,
With golden spike and glitt'ring sheen,
  Beneath it crushed a countless throng
Stifled and cramped, and still oppressed
By toilsome dreams—they do not rest.

Gaze over Europe's face, and see
  How man beneath the shadow sits
Of an ingenious tyranny
  Which shames the very Jesuits—
See plastic youth its chosen prey,
Its lesson, "Question not—obey."

The sage ball-cartridge forced to learn;
  Philanthropists the bayonet;

The great free-thinker made to turn,
  The puppet of the martinet—
The grand accomplished end sublime,
To march mankind to funeral time.

They say we *think* not (envy-twitched)—
  Perchance 'tis true. But they stand still—
Our instinct used, and boldly hitched
  To our great wain, outruns their skill.
Which gives most promise, which is best,
Unconscious speed, or conscious rest?

Columbia, sure thou hast a wing
  To bear thee far above their flight—
It may seem but a slender thing
  To one who sees not latent might—
'Tis this—Great Presence, do I err?
Thou dost not love the lawgiver.

For thou, and thou alone, art teaching
  The first great lesson for the free,
All-comprehensive and all-reaching—
  It is responsibility.
Compulsion, try, and try again,
Thou ne'er shalt frame one citizen.

II.

The snow was banked against the pane,
  Each ivy leaf its burden bore;
The last flake falling grazed the vane,
  And nestled on the roof; the roar
Of the old pines was low or loud,
As ever to the blast they bowed.

The orb which lights, but never warms,
  Like ship that leaves the land a-lee,
From forth the towering cliff-like forms
  Of the white clouds drew steadily;
Sending pale messengers below
To glimmer o'er the paler snow.

A world of white! the sailing moon,
  The clouds, the universal snow;
Fair nature lies as in a swoon,
  Pale, cold, still, beautiful—ah, how
Can scenes like this of nothingness
Our thoughts subdue, our hearts oppress?

'Tis Matter's might which bids us bow
  Before her still supremacy;
The only infinite we know,
  Cradle and grave of all we see—
Hearts quail before the eternal state
Which decks her power inanimate.

Wild Tobehanna's hemlock shades,
  Mont Vélan's pallid pyramid,
The boundless plains where blooms and fades
  The prairie rose, and where forbid
Shadows may dwell not, these all wear
The self-same strange abstracted air.

The indifference of one who reigns
  By effortless necessity,
Whose unapparent might remains
  And moulds the things that live and die,—
Of one who waits some distant day
Beyond all thought, far, far away.

Ye tortured of the earth, who deem
  Your torturers omnipotent,
Turn to the ocean, lake, the stream,
  The mountain, or the forest bent
By the free wind—nay, turn, and see
Their palsied, blind infirmity.

Ye mourners of the heart, who weep
  O'er evanescence and decay,
O'er mutual vows, which *one* did keep,
  O'er hopes now memories, flesh now clay—
Seek the inanimate, and cull
The sole bloom indestructible.

Ye victims of the mind, who pine
  To impinge upon Futurity,
Who live beyond the hour, and twine
  Your thoughts with shades of things to be,
Who faint beneath the feverish strain
To fix the phantoms of the brain,

When daily things of loathly hue
  Rise up between you and your aim,
And blot the far entrancing view
  With beckoning forms and eager claim—
To nature turn, and strive to be
Faint image of her constancy.

Look backward o'er man's trodden path,
  'Tis Matter bounds the horizon;
And save that far before he hath
  But shifting clouds to gaze upon,
Where'er he turns there meets his eye
A palpable Eternity.

His life and all it holds most dear,
  Fame, Fortune, and Philosophy,
The laugh, the jest, the rising tear,
  Calm Friendship's clasp of constancy,
And lovers' lips that warmly press,
Brief camp-fires in its wilderness.

E'en sceptics who deny thy might,
  Great Matter, worship at thy shrine;
And journey far by day and night
  To view thy fairest forms divine—
By instinct is this homage wrung
From man to that from whence he sprung.

III.

In the old armor-groaning times
  Men's life was nearer their ideal,—
A thick-set man, as shown in rhymes,
  Whose brain alone might be unreal—
Nay, smile not, for they chased their idol
With reeking spur and hanging bridle.

But our ideal is so subtle
  That few men know of its existence,
Unlike that firm fish called the cuttle,
  Which always needs the teeth's assistance;
Since all men so substantial find it
That few can eat it absent-minded.

The school Romantic is no more;
  The school grotesque, I ween, is fainting;
The hand of Fame is still before
  The new name which she now is painting—
Some letters show—perchance her scrawl
May read, THE INTELLECTUAL.

When the world's heart is purer far,
  When the world's eye is doubly clear,
When thought untrammelled, like a star,
  Above the horizon doth appear,
Shall Poetry not lift her head,
And sing the living, not the dead?

IV.

Within behold no chivalry
  Of lords and dames in proud array,
But just a simple company,
  The fleeting children of to-day,
Who now must trim in their brief turn
That lamp which doth forever burn.

A sombre hall, despite the blaze!
  The spirit of the olden time
Wandered unvanquished; yet the rays
  Did timidly but glowing climb
O'er autumn leaves embalmed, and ferns
And flowers niched in figured urns.

And to and fro were many straying,
  Absorbed and whispering as they went;
While some o'er flowers were delaying;
  Some formed in noisy groups; some bent
With their soft careless modern grace
O'er cracked wild paintings of the chase.

Upon a sofa of green leather
  Sat three who figure as examples,
As neatly clipped and pinned together
  As silks when sent to dames for samples;
One bore a look upon his brow
Which was not mindless, even now.

His aims were once beyond his powers;
  But disappointment brought contraction,
Till, aimless now, he filled his hours
  With painful sneers for those in action—
He turned his feet from side to side,
And gazed on them with thoughtful pride.

Two maidens garnished him like truffles,
  And while he gazed, in solemn thought,
They gazed on him, and through their ruffles
  Some tincture from his musings caught.
O Reader, if their conversation
Were served, 'twould prove a cold collation.

Around them, and above them all,
  There hummed a dull spasmodic sound,—
As wind-filled mantles rise and fall,
  Now swollen high, now on the ground—
Anon it ceased—a moment after,
There came a rattling peal of laughter.

Turn whence the sound proceeded most,
  And passing through an open door
Behold a mingled, motley host
  Of young and old. And still the roar
Grew louder, as some entrance new
Found welcome from the nearest few.

The lights' clear penetrating glow,
  Like to Lycurgus' flowing hair,*

_____
* It will be remembered that Lycurgus' reason for causing his
Spartans to wear long hair was that it made "the ugly more hideous
and the beautiful more lovely." This idea forms a curious contrast to
our modern notion of universal handicapping.

To all the hideous gave a blow.
     But cast a necklace on the fair,—
Light universal, overflowing
All things, and every object showing.

'Twas a great modern room whose red
     Deep-folded curtains swept the floor.
The walls were high and light, and shed
     The white blaze back again, which bore
Fresh breath and life to paintings two,
Hung opposite, one old, one new;

For light is pictures' air. The one
     Was a dark, twilight, hemlock scene:
The watery pathway of the cone
     Speeds on beneath the eternal green;
Round fallen trees and boulders gleam
The hoary eddies of the stream.

And from the torrent, ambered deep
     By mining roots of thousand pines,
Dark shadows slowly upward creep,
     Commingling as the day declines;
But on a distant wooded hill
Some rear-guard sunbeams loiter still.

Above a high, carved mantel, where
     Diana, full of idle grace,
Reclined with a voluptuous air,
     While swept afar the eager chase,
There was the likeness of a dame
Of other days, yet still the same.—

Not like old portraits ghastly gray,
  Loose hanging upon frescoed walls,
Which look as if upon the day
  When died their quaint originals,
Death swept a shadow o'er their flush,
Retouching with a colder brush—

So clear the light within her eye,
  So free the blood upon her cheek,
It seemed that she in passing by
  A window had but stopped to speak;
So that her snuff-box and quaint dress
Were startling almost to distress.

If that old portrait on the wall,
  From her high vantage-ground above,
Had gazed upon the festival,
  With a time-questioning glance which strove
To catch the spirit of the host,
On one her gaze had lingered most.

He stood amidst the thickest throng,
  And yet the mingling life which streamed
Its rays upon his being strong
  Was like the light that round him gleamed,
It could not reach his heart's deep place,
But flickering played upon his face.

For that new principle of thought
  Diffused like life through all the rest,

And yet so widely faintly wrought,
   That it in each was scarce confessed,
Had on his heart condensed, until
He owned its weight and felt its chill.

He bore no tragic look of gloom,
   No cynic's guise, by which despair
Is made a dead life to assume,
   Becoming an empoisoned air;
With interest upon all around
He turned a gaze close and profound.

It was as if he deemed mankind,
   Their thousand motives good or ill,
Were light chips by some sibyl blind
   Commingled, yet related still,
And he the fragments would compare,
And form one full mosaic fair.

He wore the air of over-thought,
   It seemed as if his strong young frame
Were strained to meet the havoc wrought
   By toiling towards some hidden aim,
Or slowly tracking skulking truth,
With endless toil, from earliest youth.

For one so young, his face was stern,
   His mouth was hard, with sharp-cut lines;
Yet through the whole a light did burn,
   Even as the firefly dimly shines
Through an illumined night-closed flower,
Soft glimmering at the twilight hour.

There was a something in his eye,
   A sense of distance in its gaze,
Which daunted near reality,
   And called back scenes of other days—
Bird-voices, clouds, and woody slopes,
Entangled with forgotten hopes.

And yet methinks, if judge I may,—
   Who should not judge, who tell the tale,—
His look and manner both betray
   A heart too absolute, too frail
In human sympathies, too prone
To make its world, and live alone.

But now, bent o'er a lady fair,
   With whisper low, he laughed as gay
As if his every thought were there
   (The vulgar only are *distrait*)—
Sudden he turned, and raised his head,
For some one at his elbow said,—

"Edmond, she sings to-night." "Who sings?"
   "Helen"—the rest was lost; for he
Who spoke passed on; the voice, like rings
   Of smoke, which rise distinct and free,
Was swept away, deprived of form,
Before the eddying wordy storm.

Then Edmond turned, with languid air,
   To a young relative near by,

And asked her if she did not care
  To fashion this celebrity,
Now formless, in his mind; she tried
To look unnettled, and replied,—

"You have not been presented, then,
  To this your hostess' guest, nor knew
That she was here—if a large wen
  Upon the marble forehead grew
Of the great statue in the square,
I doubt if you would even stare.

"How long she may intend to stay
  None know"—her eye with mischief gleams—
"You'd better ask her, by the way,
  'Twill keep you from more dangerous themes.—
She comes from" . . . sudden they both felt
Their speech into their hearing melt.

A slowly disentangling sound
  Through the thick voice of that close throng
Crept softly up, and spread around,
  Unaided, yet wild, clear, and strong;
For no accompaniment was there,
Save the vibration of the air.

That sweet ungovernable tone
  Rose up as silvery bubbles rise
Through heavy waters, till alone
  It filled all ears with paradise.
With growing confidence she sang—
This song through sudden stillness rang:

The moon with her viewless hands,
Transparent, light, and free,
  Was parting a place
  For her dreamy face
To gaze on the troubled sea.

There were bells in wave-washed hands
Which tolled eternally;
  There was roar on roar
  Far down the shore,
And laughter out to sea,

There were four on the sands to-night,
Two shadows and two forms—
  Behind and before
  Flew the froth on the shore
And foam on the land of storms.

Need shadows or shapes more light?
O which has the firmer home?
  Which stabler stuff,
  The moth-like fluff,
Or the bird-like flying foam?

O heart-uniting kiss!
O bosoms beating free!
  O eye-lids wet
  With joy! and yet—
The wild bells out to sea!

Through the languor of the kiss
Which wrapped them tenderly
  Came the steady roar
  Far down the shore,
And the laughter out to sea.

Her voice's fingers ceased to sweep
   That harp aërial, thousand stringed,
Viewless and vast, which yet can keep
   No sound, though all by it are winged;
First plaudits came, but no one stirred,
And then a sudden hush was heard.

There was an essence in the tone
   As of a subtle, thought-fed flame,
By which a glimmering light was thrown
   On their past lives; till each one came
To see how far his path had strayed
From hopes which once his being made.

Before life's stream above them rolling
   Had turned them round and round and round,
Their thoughts and wishes all controlling,
   Till by its current they were ground
To an unvarying shape and hue,
Cheating the search for beauty new.

Like paltry mice that gnaw the dead,
   Each sight of the world's power, each sigh
Of stifled hope or wakened dread,
   Will eat away identity.
Each day our saliencies doth cull,
As thorny trees catch flocks of wool.

There was a something in the tone
   Which made all feel "How sweet to think,—

To be one instant all alone,
   And seeming into being sink"—
A moment more, the waves closed in
With an augmented, boisterous din.

All felt relieved to be once more
   Upon well-known, well-trodden ground:
And each bethought him of his store
   Of current pleasantries; and found
That, unawares, a thought-immersion
Had chilled, till then, his self-assertion.

But unto Edmond, in the tone
   There rang an echo of his thought:
Although to her who sang unknown,
   Like wind through clouds, there was inwrought
Throughout a chafing 'gainst constraint,
And freedom from all earthly taint.

His air indifferent, which made
   Him many an enemy, was gone.
He crossed the room; the words were said
   Which form acquaintance' neutral dawn;
He sat as near as he might dare,
With a familiar, playful air.

There was not, as romancers love,
   A sudden flashing forth of mind,
A single sentence deftly wove
   In which their life-thoughts were entwined—
Romantic reader, be not hurt,
The truth is, they began to flirt.

What contrast! she with golden hair,
   Dark eyes, and all-pervading grace—
He gray-eyed, dark as she was fair,
   And with a stern, medallion face,
Bearing an inward look which lay
Beneath his features' ceaseless play.

Their lips were active, and their eyes
   Interpreted their speech aright;
They felt an inner glad surprise,
   A thrill ecstatic, and a might,
A consciousness of power to please,
Which made excitement, mixed with ease.

They scarcely marked the words they said;
   But she was conscious that he took
Her fan, and twirled it round, and made
   Each pert speech bear a tender look.
While they are laughing at a jest
Of moderate worth, glance at the rest.

Alas! the female rank and file
   With drooping hands and eyes that wandered,
And many a weary studied smile,
   Sat emblems of existence squandered;
Each guarded by some near relation—
Sad victims of false education.

A bore (though that is scarce distinctive,
   Since all bore all except themselves)

Save those endowed with wits instinctive)
  Was ransacking his empty shelves,
And holding one impatience-mad,
Who just had spied a careless lad

Of twice his beauty, half his age,
  And versed in every amorous wile,
With his betrothed—O gods of rage!
  She bent low with a blushing smile!
Thrice had his heart transfixed the bore—
Relief came from the opening door.

A man whose waistcoat mocked his face,
  A statue cut in chocolate,
Flung wide the door with easy grace,
  And with a smile and air elate—
His potent wordless look let loose
The flood-gates of the gastric juice.

And each one gently led away
  A softly simpering sylph, to where
There gleamed a silver-loaded tray,
  While round it spread the sumptuous fare;
In dual order all marched in,
Each popping cork their culverin.

v.

Below, the house is still and dark,
  And all above, save that between

The long lace curtains, like a spark,
 A dim and lonely light is seen,
Where more than one fair girlish guest,
With her from far, prepares for rest.

Pink shoulders glisten glazed and round,
 And many a flaccid garment white
Is held from slipping to the ground
 By elbows jealous of the sight
Of the full hip and loosened waist
Through their thin drapery dimly traced.

Young laughter low fills all the room;
 And Raillery, Youth's friend, with naught
To mark him, save a fragile broom,
 To brush away the seeds of thought,
Controls each light heart beating fast
With memories of the revel past.

As gay as if the tree of life
 No shadow cast athwart the world,
A thousand questions mischief-rife,
 All fling at each; full deftly hurled,
A hail of malice lightly pays
Those whom the evening crowned with bays.

But when on Helen turns the stream
 Of girlish jests she hoped would pass,
Her eyes shoot forth an angry gleam—
 She turns away—and though she was
The loudest there but just before,
Says least—perchance to dream the more.

CANTO II.

I.

THE fairest hour of all the year!
   A winter's early afternoon:
The sky was blue, the air was clear;
   A tint half pink and half maroon,
Crept up above the horizon,
Despite the feeble western sun.

The happiest hour of all the year,
   Which frees the heart and fires the eye,
While on the cheek of health appear
   The colors of its evening sky;
With avarice we breathe the air,
So pure, transparent, cold, and rare.

A spell to wring care from the brow!
   'Tis ere the twilight hath begun,
While fir-tree shadows darker grow,
   And hill-tops redden in the sun,
To whirl across the glittering ice,
With swinging foot and rare device.

II.

She sat beside a window high,
   The central casement of the pile;
She marked the cloudless, deep blue sky,
   And Nature's cold and marble smile—
The very spirit of the year,
So beautiful it was not drear.

Before her stretched the snowy lawn,
  A valley 'twixt the towering pines;
And where some giant limb was gone
  The sunlight streamed in serried lines
Across the dry and frosty snow,
With lengthening forms and deepening glow.

By Winter's hand alone revealed,
  The distant village street was seen;
Beyond a mead in part concealed,
  Its windows caught the western sheen;
And nearer rose a maple tall,
Whose leaves are golden in the Fall.

Upon the mead a spring-house old,
  With rotted roof and fallen beam,
Lay slowly sinking in the mould,
  And choked by refuse of the stream;
Beside it Indian canes were massed,
Which hummed and whistled in the blast.

There, too, were ancient water-willows,
  And at their feet a tender spring,
Whose gentle flow and tiny billows
  Beneath the ice went murmuring.
Near by, there stood a sun-dial old,
With signs and figures manifold.

She gazed upon the wintry scene,
  And not upon the things around;

The curtains, with their figures green
　Embroidered on a sombre ground,
Came sweeping round her, rich and warm,
And almost hid her yielding form.

It was no room—but on the stair
　There was a landing deep and broad,
Windowed, room-like, luxurious; there
　Were carpets springing as the sod;
The sofa in the deep alcove
Seemed even designed for scenes of love:

For it was wide enough for two,
　And yet so narrow that the fair
Who nestled in that seat with you
　Must brush your forehead with her hair;
And o'er your cheek her soft breath straying
Made it a pleasure there delaying.

Around were mummies of the air,
　On mossy perch set stark and high,
Two owls with strange and glassy stare,
　A jay-bird, too, in act to fly—
And more of such slight straw-like things
To which the drowning memory clings.

A sketch and some engravings rare,—
　Quaint, costly vases filled with flowers,—
And, framed, a lock of snow-white hair,
　Pale, long-enduring tomb of hours
That lie afar; a table, too,
With books of every size and hue.

Thin pamphlets upon Atheism,
  To prove his eye-teeth now are cut;
Fat tomes to show how faith the schism
  Between the churches soon must shut—
With novels, too, for women's reading,
Where Love must always think of breeding.

And this, "Who lives must vote,"—and this,
  "The Prussian system as a blessing";
Near by, in an unloving kiss,
  The Westminster and British pressing—
The whole an emblem of society
Befuddled out of all sobriety.

He's like a dog with a new master,
  The old one fading from his view,
He moves now slower, and now faster,
  Now sits him down with head askew;
To follow which he scarce can tell,
Yet limps along with whine and yell.

Her rounded, half-reclining form,
  Her leaning head and sweeping tress,
Her skin so white and colors warm,
  Her foot in peeping carelessness,
All made a sight so fair, the eye
Grows dim to think such things must die.

Her mien was sad, for she was still—
  The face at rest is always sad—

Her thoughts were careless of her will,
  And strayed afar—perchance she had
Some vision faint of Edmond there,—
For who can tell? he, too, was fair.

And then they had so often met
  Since that first eve, and many an hour
She had listened almost with regret
  To his low voice's thrilling power,
Still questioning accepted things,
And seeking for life's secret springs.

New creatures of the mind, a throng
  That called him master, when he spoke
Came rushing forth and swept along
  Terribly beautiful, while broke
And fled in cloudy volumes curled
The old opinions of the world.

And when he ceased, and ere the flood
  Of daily life had swept between
And blurred his words, fair Helen stood
  In a new world of nobler mien,
Or so it seemed; for blooming there
Was Freedom's rose, and on the air

Its incense magical.—That unplucked flower
  Which is the moral Alpine rose,
And blooms where highest mountains tower;
  Still smiling o'er the awful snows
And lofty ledges wrapt in sleet,
Which check man's climbing, bleeding feet.

It seemed the world must sure be changed—
　　And yet a moment hence she saw
The idols he had shattered ranged
　　In potent state, without a flaw,
While all around her bowed the knee,
And boasted of their dignity.

And thus the contest in her mind
　　'Twixt what *seemed* true and what *was* strong,—
A feeling also scarce defined
　　That all that's sweetest *must* be wrong,—
Her thoughts in strange confusion kept,
Like reeds by eddying breezes swept.

Perchance, although she knew it not,
　　What most of all her fancy led
Was earnestness which self forgot
　　In all he thought, in all he said—
A man of any strong belief
Is now a striking *haut-relief*.

What wonder if a thought of him
　　Should ever and anon appear,
Now as a starlight shadow dim,
　　Now close beside her strong and clear,
Yet so accompanied that the eye
Still failed to mark its frequency?

She sat unconscious of the hour
　　That brushed her with its downy wing,

And swept beyond—it had no power
  To deal upon so fair a thing;
But with its airy pinions fanned
The foliage of her fairy-land.

Her eyes, though moveless as her form,
  Breathed not the same abandonment,
They imaged back now calm, now storm,
  On ever-changing shapes intent—
Unearthly mirrors where each thought
In sublimated form was wrought.

They were not large, but purest brown,
  And clearer than the mountain spring—
They had a look, 'twas all their own,
  A look of earnest lingering,
As of a softness scarce revealed,
By high unconquered pride concealed.

As to the mountain spring 'tis given
  To image every change above,
Till it becomes an earthly heaven,
  So every phase from scorn to love,
The soul's whole history, from her eyes
Flashed forth, a living Paradise.

They were not lustrous, swimming orbs,
  Of timid heart and vain desire,
Whose cloudy brilliancy absorbs
  And dissipates the inner fire—
They had a tingeless beam divine,
As stars when viewed from mountains shine.

III.

A foot-fall on the winding stair!
  She heard it not, but gazed without;
Yet Edmond stood beside her there,
  While restless roamed his glance about,
Till suddenly it fell upon
The thing he sought—his breath was gone.

His parted lips were still as clay,
  And one foot slowly backward stepped,
As it would bear his form away;
  While o'er his cheek a pallor crept,
Gray as the dews of early morn,
That glisten on September's corn—

Faint as the blue in moonlight, or
  The tint upon a sea-flower's cheek,
Or shapes of trees and shrubs before
  The morn begins the East to streak—
'Twas faint as all of these, yet clear—
'Twas early love's companion—fear.

Upon a wild and blooming mead
  Whoe'er has stopped, and looked behind,
Has seen the flowers from 'neath his tread
  Rise slowly up, though still inclined—
So slowly did he gain control
Of his bewildered, panting soul.

With leaded feet, but steady mien,
  He crossed in silence from the stair,
And glided to her side unseen,
  And with a half-caressing air
Sat down beside her in the groove
Of the old panelled deep alcove.

She started—and a wingèd cry
  Sprang to her lips, but rested there;
For turning quick she met his eye—
  And o'er her face, confused but fair,
There rippled forth a sudden blush,
With far diffused and spreading flush.

As welcome to that gazer's eye,
  In tint as lovely, as the rose
Which first beholds June's deep blue sky,
  While comrades still are in repose;
Whom kissing dews have waked, with fear
To be the season's pioneer.

Her color deepened, as she laughed
  With beautiful embarrassment;
But even now excitement's graft,
  From fear, the trunk on which it leant,
Had sprouted wild—in mutual tease
And jest, they felt—no not at ease,—

But a sweet fever, a desire
  To push each other towards the brink;

With icy hands and head on fire,
    They trifle, showing, though they shrink,
That trembling eagerness which gives
To light words power o'er human lives.

Perchance their limbs e'en lightly touched—
    They knew it not, or if they did,
The happy senses quickly clutched
    Perception's robe, and gently bid
Her turn and look another way,
Which she did willingly obey.

Unconsciously their eyes began
    To gain a deeper, softer light,
A tremor through their being ran,
    Their world seemed fuller, and a might
Voluptuous languished in each vein—
'Twas like the quick surcease of pain.

Unconsciously their voices fell
    Lower and lower, till the tone
Was like the tremble of a bell
    When the stroke ceases; there alone,
They felt their horizon expand,
Like one who finds an unknown land.

Her hand is at her lover's lips,
    Cold as a flower before the dawn—
He breathes, as from his clasp it slips,
    "You love me?" Turning towards the lawn
And rivalling its sunset glow,
She whispers, "I could love"—when lo!

The banister, that friend to age,
   Gave forth a sudden creaking sound,—
The steps groaned as in fear and rage,—
   A smothered wheezing upward wound,—
A heavy foot toiled up the stair—
An inmate elderly was there!

Their breath was short from passion—hers
   From her late combat with the stairs;
And as she slow removed her furs
   She talked of thousand trifles—theirs
It was to stand with flashing eyes
And burning cheeks, and blurt replies.

How much the small round eyes might see
   They knew not, scarcely cared—their hope
Was from the presence to be free,
   And give their prisoned feelings scope—
But pretexts fly from scenes of flurry,
As shirt-buttons from scenes of hurry

At last, with unremembering mien,
   Helen remembered that that day
She had not once the green-house seen—
   The sun was low—she feared the gray,
Long, winter shadows would confuse
Its tints, and blur the flowers' hues.

And thus they hastened forth, when he
   Had first around her wrapped a shawl,

Dark, fringed, and broidered curiously—
    They stood within the antlered hall—
Around her slow he drew its fold
With lingering fingers scarce controlled.

And as he drew his hands away,
    Perchance they swept the full round form,
As lightly as a snow-flake may
    A leaf which trembles in the storm—
And Helen trembled, while her cheek
Was like that leaflet's crimson streak.

Along the snow-cut walk they passed
    'Twixt lines of peeping box—their eyes
Were downcast, and their hearts beat fast—
    Their forms were colored by the skies.
Slow grew their steps as on they went,
White-breathed, sun-tinted, forward bent.

IV.

A moment leave them, if but one—
    Their feelings who can separate?
Self-consciousness was almost gone,
    Save a strange heart-gripe, half elate—
A painful waking into life
Of hopes and fears, of calm and strife.

A moment follow Edmond's thought
    In its involuntary range.

In vain to rouse himself he sought,
    Against his will the scene would change—
His mind flagged, overtaxed and strained—
The past upon his footsteps gained.

He stands, as oft a boy he stood,
    In Pennsylvania's wilderness—
A clearing in a mighty wood
    Whose dark ranks on it seem to press;
Around the sumach gleams like fire,
Massed thick with wild-flowers, brush, and brier.

And underneath the sumach's red,
    Its brown and furry branch is seen,
Like deer-horns in the velvet; dead
    And lichen-coated stumps between
Peep dully forth; and over all,
With golden slant, in patches fall

Warm Autumn sunbeams, populous
    With darting moths, and poisèd flies,
And clustered gnats all nebulous;
    Amidst, a barkless tree doth rise,
Upon whose forked and pointed limbs
The reddening sunlight slowly climbs.

The outlaw hawk his watch-tower finds
    Upon its topmost branch, so still
He seems a branch, save that the winds
    Oft raise his feathers like a frill.
Who looks aright upon such scenes
Upon a power immortal leans.

'Twas but a twitching of the brain,
　　A flash of the o'erwilful mind,
A consciousness akin to pain,—
And yet in words how slow defined—
Thoughts have an eye which all things sees,
But words feel on by slow degrees.

v.

How tangled on the warm moist air,
　　The perfumes of a thousand flowers!
The blooms of an acacia fair
　　Fell down in meteoric showers,
As they, unmindful, jarred the door,
And paced the raised and latticed floor.

They joined the beauty of the scene,
　　A part unconscious, even as those
Whose many-colored ranks between
　　They slowly passed; the gentle blows
Of overhanging petalled sprays
Could not awake their outward gaze.

Pale callas and azaleas white,
　　And heliotropes flashed ruby-hued
In the long-threaded, deep red light
　　With which their fibres seemed imbued—
Save only the outrivalled rose,
Which sank into a pale repose.

The young flood of their lives has come!
　　The pathway to one side was bent

At the end of the long glassy dome—
  Here Helen turned, and turning leant,
With grace which turmoil could not dim,
Upon the old wall's wood-bound rim.

Her eyes flashed full upon her lover,
  But sank as quickly to the ground,
As if his thoughts she would discover,
  Yet feared an import too profound—
A moment Edmond silent stood,
Then spoke in concentrated mood.

"You know I love you—words are vain
  To paint the passion in my breast,
Yet must I say it o'er again,
  And o'er, and o'er until oppressed
By joy—one only thought is clear,
'Tis I who speak and you who hear.

"For the mere breathing of this word,
  Its simple utterance twixt us twain,
E'en though but for a moment heard,
  Forges a mystic, viewless chain,
A mutual knowledge hid from all,
Which time and change can ne'er recall.

"The sense that there exists a link
  Between a thing so fair and me,
I feel,—for now I cannot think,—
  Is joy as boundless as the sea;
I feel new force within my frame,
My being is not all the same.

"I boast no pure platonic flame,
    No spiritual love divine,
My heart I cannot, would not tame,
    To prate with desultory whine,
Of disembodied souls united
And ghosts in holy union plighted.

"What is a love that sex denies?
    'Tis friendship, liking, what you will,
Aught, anything but love —it lies,
    And calls itself a prince; but still
Forgets its part, and asks for alms,
With abject mien and shaking palms.

"Nay, 'tis a pale and jaundiced thing
    Born of a sickly phantasy,
Suspicious, ready to take wing,
    And feeding but on vanity—
A thing that waits and bides its time—
But patience is love's greatest crime.

"The brutal peasant's dull desire,
    The dreamer's chilly preference,
Are peers—but oh! the living fire,
    Still fed by soul, and fanned by sense,
This, this is love, and it is mine—
Oh, may I whisper, Is it thine?

"My eyes like things within a net,
    Can never struggle from your charms,

I—nay, I *will* be bold—and yet—
   I die to press you in my arms,
To feel the beauty that I see,
And worship its reality.

"You hear me; oh! the boon is much—
   Yet would you quickly shrink away,
Recoiling from my lightest touch,
    Like ripples from the breezes play,
Or struggling endmost leaves,—or rills,
Or echoes, springing from the hills.

"It is no hour for measured speech,
   Yet ere yon ruddy clouds grow gray
With early age, I fain would teach
    You what I am. How hard to say
That which may—No, when on the brink,
Upon the gulf 'tis death to think.

"I ne'er shall deem, as deems the world,
   That woman is a drifting thing,
Meant but to float with sails all furled
    And rotting useless where they cling,
While others skim along the deep,
And toward the far horizon sweep.

"I could not treat you as a child,
   To be cajoled, deceived, caressed,
Deluded, dazzled, and beguiled,
    By silken, jewelled cords oppressed—
No, no, I love you! hear and see
The truth, and choose your destiny.

"Oft would I leave my comrades' play
   To follow morning mists on high,
Swift ghostly guides which swept away
   Towards the mountain-tops, while I
Toiled after them, until I gained
Gulf-peering rocks, whose necks seemed strained—

"Serrate, snow-sifted, awful things,
   Forgetful of their nature,—striving
With outstretched beak and stony wings
   To fly from the bleak summits,—living
Chained by one foot alone—while under
Roll unopposed blasts, clouds and thunder.

"No life was there, save thoughts that dwell
   In airy desolation—these
Made populous the cliffs, the dell
   Shrunk to a shade, the adventurous trees
Which clung beneath, the distance that
Pillared my feet while there I sat.

"Oft did my childish footsteps roam
   Where lives the otter, turtle, eel,—
The widgeon's and the black-duck's home,—
   Wild sedges of the snipe and teal,—
Those boundless marshes green and fair,
Which fringe the mighty Delaware.

"The red-winged blackbird singing swung
   Upon a low-bent reed; near by

A cat-tail o'er the water hung,
  And dipped, and dipped, and constantly
Let fall one drop, whose life expanded
In circles dying ere they stranded.

"And I—I gazed, and gazed, and dreamed,
  So still the musk-rat brushed me by;
Above me far the fish-hawk screamed,
  The buzzard floated in the sky;
While in my heart rose thoughts profound,
The children of the scenes around.

"I dared to dream of Liberty—
  She seemed in Nature's image framed,
But with a fairer destiny—
  Like her all boundless and untamed,
And like her ne'er to know surcease.
Yet, unlike her, still to increase.

"I dared to think—I think so still—
  That man o'erburdened cannot climb,—
That man may, must obey his will,
  His compass on the sea of time—
That needle true which from afar
Still points towards Progress' polar star.

"There is a freedom higher still
  Than that which takes embodied form
In states that own the people's will,
  And keep the hopes of millions warm—
It is the freedom of the mind,
Whose limits ne'er shall be defined.

"It is the right conferred by Thought
    On him who wears her cognizance—
An hour, with this motto wrought,
    I cannot turn, but must advance—
To act upon his heart's behest,
His own tribunal in his breast.

"I gaze across the moving world,
    And see one stationary thing,—
Still as a winter's leaf all curled
    And cold upon the breast of Spring—
Oh, why must woman live beneath
The shadow grim of moral death?

"What is her life from infancy?
    To be the chosen ward of age—
That stolid guard with leaden eye,
    Who hints no life beyond her cage—
So trained to darkness that her sight
Shrinks aching from a ray of light.

"She is the sport of words, the scene
    Of life's most lifeless tragedy,
The shuttlecock which flies between
    Prescription and Propriety;
Her thoughts are hamstrung as they rise,
Her hopes are smothered spite their cries.

"O'er the world's snow her instincts peering,
    Bright hyacinths of her new-born Spring,

Their petals innocently rearing,
  And timidly as they would cling
To a stray sunbeam, sink 'neath feet
Which wait their forms in pulp to beat.

"But what are woman's rights? To bear
  The brunt of life's necessities?
In toil and progress both to share?
  Ay; but her right eternal is,
To love when, how, and whom she would—
Her chains are on her womanhood.

"The modern man—not him of old,
  Who stalks about in modern dress—
That human flesh is bought and sold
  Can never learn; companionless,
He moves amongst a captive throng
Whose thoughts do not to them belong.

"They say that woman loves the grave,
  That she is with her lot content,
As lately 'gainst another slave,
  Now free, the self-same bow was bent—
This is their argument: the lower
The fire, the less it needs the blower.

"There is a feeling in the world,
  A ghost from the long-buried past,
That life would be in chaos hurled,
  If hearts were not in irons cast—
Then progress is thy fruit, O tree,
Swift fading now, of tyranny!

"The laws on usury and trade
  Were deemed the guardians of mankind—
Where are they? Yet their loss has made
  The liens which modern life doth bind—
Does then the nobler part, the soul,
More than self-interest need control?

"As men place screws in coffin-lids—
  Place to remain—Opinion makes
Youth's heart a fixity—then chides
  Its still cold dream which never wakes—
That ships may quickly come to land,
Pray nail the compass to its stand."

He turned to her and faintly smiled,—
  A trembling smile;—thus far the flow
Of his own passion had beguiled
  The crisis of his thoughts: but now—
He sudden gazed into her eyes,
Yet saw no clear-drawn answer rise.

She looked the feeling in her heart,
  'Twas that of one, who from some deep
And gentle dream awaked in part,
  Would back into the vision creep—
He nearer drew, and 'gan to speak
With softer voice and paler cheek.

"The world would drive me from your side,
  To seek the lowly and the vile—

For only wealth can take a bride,
  On him alone 'dare beauty smile—
Or I must wait and toil till I
Can smother love in luxury.

"What, must I wait as Youth now waits,
  Deep in the selfish search for gain,
His hands, but not his heart the State's,
  Careless of others' joy or pain,
Dead to all public thought?—O men!
Why is not Youth a citizen?

"Oh, must I live, like Youth, a priest
  In all but hood and shaven crown,—
One of a caste apart,—released
  From that sweet bond round others thrown,
With no bright chain of sympathy
And love between mankind and me?

"Or may I dream that life is fair
  And pure as latticed moonlight? We
But note the image it may wear
  To us. Can you repeat with me,
O Virtue! thou art guileless love?
May not our hearts in concert move?

"Oh, can you love me as I am?"
  She tore a flower to yellow spray,
And faltered, "In my own room's calm,
  I have so much that I would say,
So much to tell; but when you come,
I know not why, yet I am dumb.

"And now, 'twere foolish to deny
   That aught that you have said has found
My heart—to answer I would try—
   But I have thoughts which will not sound—
Perhaps, if I could once begin—
'Tis growing late—we will go in."

Her voice had ever thrilled his heart,
   Liquid and sweet, yet free in tone;
But now no language could impart
   Its trembling life, before unknown.
In all the world there can be found
To match with it one only sound—

'Tis robins' voices, after showers,
   When sudden bursts the setting sun
Upon the dripping leaves and flowers,
   And robes them in his mantle dun—
Hark how their chorus wild and clear
Sweeps throught the freshened atmosphere!

With no endearment, no embrace,
   No pressure of the hand, they turned
Their footsteps slowly to retrace;
   But on each cheek a lustre burned,
Their step was firmer, and their eye
Flashed faith on treacherous Destiny.

They were as dew-drops which condense
   From out the universal air,—

Each mortal's breath, but more intense,—
  A part of what is everywhere—
These flash in heaven's own light arrayed,
Then vanish ere their colors fade.

They were bright ripples of that river
  Which rushes through the human mind,
That stream which sweeps along forever,
  Whose gathering volume naught can bind—
Foam from its current, with a gleam,
Still eddying onward while we dream.

CANTO III.

I.

In the wild sea-goat's coil the moon
  Hung low upon the Southern bord;
The trees' long shadows crept to noon
  Upon their dial of dusky sward.—
Sleep, shadows, sleep, forget to move,
Spare the returnless hours of love.

There was no wind, yet sable clouds,
  With moon-lit garments white and fair,
Swept slowly on; not massed in crowds,
  But one by one, with pensive air,
As if their noiseless feet kept time
To some wild strain, unheard, sublime.

The cricket sang his August song,
  His still-recurring ghostly glee—
A tone which makes a moment long,
  And images Eternity;
Making new stillness, even where
There is no sound, no breath of air.

Naught marred that harmony of gloom
  Which follows dying Summer's days.
The grasshopper his threadless loom
  Had checked as sank the western rays;
The rattling locust's scorching cry
Had ceased while yet the sun was high.

The maple leaves their silvered side
   Turned outward to the moon; for they
Yielded to a quick gust, which died
   Almost before they could obey,—
Leaving no currents where it passed,
Those airy footprints of the blast.

It was no midnight damp and chill
   Such as late August ever knows,
When night feels a cold shuddering thrill
   While dreaming of the coming snows;
'Twas June, without her spirits high,
And intermittent fire-fly.

The silent, ivy-shrouded mansion
   By contrast seemed as ghostly white
As when on buttress, roof, and stanchion
   The snow was piled that winter's night;
For shades corporeal from each tree
Replaced their netted filigree.

Across a narrow path which skirted
   A chasm deep where willows grew,—
By daylight lonely and deserted,—
   The branches tangled shadows threw;
And where they fell not, gleamed the grass
And diamond-glitt'ring isinglass.

From out the weed-encumbered dell,
   Tier upon tier along its bank,

Trees rose with undulating swell,
   Like wave on wave; a figure shrank
Within the border of the glade,
Where densest fell the ebon shade.

'Tis Edmond; for a moonbeam now
   Flits o'er his face—an instant there,—
Yet long enough, alas! to show
   Already that pain, doubt, and care,
Love's train, have made his heart their home—
No more, mayhap, from there to roam.

Doubts of himself, his life, his mind,
   Of the close-woven thoughts of years,
Doubts of all freedom, of mankind—
   Such doubts assailed him and such fears,
As o'er the world in parties steal,
And ever on the wounded deal.

"Is life but our own heart with wings?
   Our deepest theories fretting games,
One long mistake of thoughts for things,
   A mingling of uncertain names?
And all our efforts but the one
To gain the hazy horizon?

"The hope to find a love which may
   Those forces into being call
Which we feel dormant in our clay,
   These are not more chimerical—
A happy man, a singing flower,
A sailing stone, a generous power."

His thoughts limped slowly, sadly on:
  "She comes not; I have overweighed
Each word, each look, and every one
  Of the impassioned hours which made
Recoil seem but a mockery—
They melt beneath my very eye.

"I know she loves me; but her heart
  Has failed. And now, what end, what key
To all which had become a part
  Of my own life! to stand and see
The moonbeams frost the hemlock cone,
And hear this summer wind—alone."

A sinewy step, but light as down!
  A quick form glanced from shade to shade—
A stifling net seemed round him thrown—
  Where fled his thoughts of love betrayed?
Sudden his blood reversed its flow—
Helen is on his bosom now!

The embrace seemed as 'twould last forever,
  Yet was the coldest of their lives—
'Twas only the untaught endeavor
  To catch at aught that respite gives.
They felt it soon must end, and then—
Trembling they closer drew again.

She raised her head and gazed around,
  As if seized by some outward fear—

They heard a rustling on the ground,
  Because they knew no life was near;
Each felt an inmost dread to own
That they were thus all, all alone.

They turned and slowly paced along,
  And as they moved beneath the trees,
Leaf-shadows, clustered throng on throng,
  Swept up their garments, until these
Dim shapes appeared a dreamy flood
Still hurrying o'er them while they stood.

And as they went, there oft recurred
  The self-same questions and replies,—
If aught within the house had stirred,
  And why she came so late—their eyes
Met not—she answered all was still,
Like one in sleep deprived of will.

Had they not striven to be alone?
  Had they not planned this hour from far?
And now—they could but check a moan,
  And gazing on each tranquil star,
Strive from its beam some thought to gain
To still their hearts, which throbbed to pain.

There was a bench beneath some willows,
  Which, as the lovers sought their shade,
Above them rolled their foamless billows;
  They gained this small and open glade;
Unconsciously he spread her cloak;
They sat them down, but neither spoke.

A silver birch erect and fair
  Its multitudinous shadow cast
Even at their feet, and lingering there,
  The moon a white band round it passed;
Its trembling shades fixed Helen's eye—
She dared not move, yet knew not why.

This was their summer home by day,
  No leaf was there they had not seen,
Yet all seemed strange, and far away—
  Their past as if it had not been;
They almost wished they had not come,—
Each strove to speak, yet both were dumb.

They sat as they would sit forever
  Parts of the scene inanimate,
Like Egypt's sitting forms which never
  Their awful stillness shall abate;
The moonlight checkered each pale face,
And lighted their dim resting-place.

From out that all-surrounding deep,
  That silent, phantom-peopled clime,
That void where all our feelings sleep
  Till they are by the watchman Time
Called into waking, there arose
In Edmond, something like repose.

With effort, but untrembling now,
  He passed his arm about her form;

His heart grew sentient; flow on flow,
  From that resistance soft and warm,
A nascent glow began to creep
Through all his being waked from sleep.

Their heart-beat changed—it swifter grew,—
  Nay, swift to suffocation, yet
'Twas steady as an infant's, who
  In sleep hath nothing to forget;
They almost laughed with joy to hear
Fall clinking down the chains of fear.

As when in some wild-cadenced chant
  The deep bass sudden volume gives,
So now in every breath they pant
  A fulness comes from their past lives,
Which bodying this hour's soul,
Gives passionate meaning to the whole.

There, in the old, scooped rustic seat,
  With willow sweepers round them twining,
Their warm hearts feel each other's beat,
  No moonbeams are between them shining,
They cast one shade. Your longings slake,
E'en Time treads lighter for your sake!

Oh, how it happened who can tell?
  The love-opposing brooch, which bound
With prudish clasp her robe, now fell,
  And glistened down upon the ground;
Her bosom flashed forth full and white—
Then deeply dyed the pale moonlight.

Not the moon's liquid marble flood,
　Like tombstones melted and diffused,
Could steal the hue from that young blood,
　Whose rush her senses all confused;
Her head sank down upon his breast,
As birds at sunset seek their rest.

Nature's dim mantle wrapped them round,
　And her soft prompting breath, by day
Far scattered o'er the world like sound,
　Urging to love all living clay,
Even to the mites on each flower's stem;
Now that all slept, fell full on them;

And in their glance of languid light,
　Their failing muscles and their frames,
Which tingled with a pained delight,
　The struggled utterance of their names,
In their sigh, as they backward leant,
It found one wild embodiment.

II.

'Tis moonset, and the trees among
　The moonlight pours, an altered thing,
It has a life, a spirit tongue
　The senses all bewildering;
A dreamy splendor reigns whose hue
Makes pale the real and the true.

The moon shines from the Western bord,
  As only sinking moons can shine;
While flashes back from the wet sward
  A glow like phosphorescent brine;
Instead of white beams cold and tame,
Behold one widespread yellow flame.

The trees' black shadows sleep in files,
  Like cloak-wrapped corpses on the field,
Between them long illumined aisles
  Stretch Eastward. Oh, fair dreamers, yield,
Before this radiance soft awake!
Ere Time your bubble rudely break.

Despite the beauty of the hour,
  Which wooes their concentrated gaze,
Despite the waning night's chill power,
  Which fain would cool their blood's bright blaze,
They dream, as they together press,
If dreaming be forgetfulness.

Melt into moonlight if ye may!
  While Nature beats your impulses,
While she is near you, and her sway
  Finds form in yon transfusing kiss,—
While every intermediate thought,
And man-born influence is naught.

Melt into moonlight if ye may!
  Behold, it widely round you gleams,

On every leaf, each glistening spray,
  Each dew-bent blade of grass it streams,
While softer rays twined with your hair,
Form halos like the moon doth wear.

Melt into moonlight if ye may!
  Oh, leave not soft indulgent Night!
Towards you floating with the day
  Comes the harsh world, whose monster might
Still rises with the sun's red car,
But pales before the rising star.

III.

The moon with every hindmost beam
  And all her shadowy train was gone,
Like some bright, many-thoughted dream,
  Which flies at the approach of dawn;
But o'er the farthest Western hill
A golden memory lingered still.

The middle heaven still was blue,
  But opposite, within the east,
There rose a bright-green matchless hue
  Pale with the thoughts of conquest; beast
And bird, and every living thing
Felt tremors stir their slumbering.

The winter stars, which told of morn,
  Were high above the horizon;

They wore an aspect lost and lorn,
   As if they saw the coming sun—
How different from the glances clear
With which they rise to rule the year!

The beings we have followed far
   Awoke, but not from sleep, to feel
A motion new within life's car—
   But whither? Though their senses reel,
A new thought thrills them—it is this,—
A longer, slower, softer kiss.

The freshness of the early morn,
   The dream-notes of still slumbering birds,
The fragrance of the tasselled corn,
   Unconscious mingled with their words,
And tempered their wild hearts' excess
With an o'erflow of tenderness.

Now all unchecked, her head sank down,
   And seemed to melt into his breast,
While languidly about him thrown,
   Her white arms hung, and she was pressed
Close to his heart,—but yet both shook
And eastward cast a troubled look.

They parted, 'tis enough to say—
   What matter how? at last 'twas done.
They slowly forced their forms away,
   Their backward glances, one by one,
They loosened from their hold, till these
Were baffled by the misty trees.

O Future! whatsoe'er thou hast
  For them within thy changing clime,
Thou never canst excel the past—
  Oh, let them stay the hand of Time!
While their young life-twig still is seen
An Autumnless, bright, living green.

Green as the moss on fallen trees
  In Susquehanna's wooded valleys,
Where sunbeams come not, and the breeze
  But with the topmost branches dallies;
Where all is moist, where all is still,
Save the crow's rasp, and trickling rill.

Turn from the hues our life doth wear,
  From love, and joy, and fear, and hope,
Which are but varied names for care,
  To that which gives our spirit scope—
See, Pennsylvania widely spreads
Her hemlock forest o'er our heads.

Ascend yon hill of sloping green—
  A leafy ocean rolls below
Its timeless flood, and brightly sheen
  Its billows as the breezes blow;
By day 'tis weird, mysterious, dim,—
By night black, spirit-filled and grim.

The deep, slow laughter of a bird,*
  With its wild, marrow-seeking thrill,

---

* It has been the writer's good fortune to hear the great laughing owl under the circumstances described. There is no mocking malice in the laugh. That were commonplace. It is the blood-curdling indifference to all human weal or woe of the deep tones, as they slowly die away, which makes them so terrible.

At midnight and by moonlight heard,
  Far sweeping through the shadows chill,
Clutches the 'lated passer's heart—
Then hurls it onward with a start.

Who could not dream his woes away,
  Fair Pennsylvania, by thy pools
Black with the blood of pines, and gray
  With stumps of perished trees; where rules
A painless stillness of the tomb,
A happy, heart-sustaining gloom.

Each heart that mingles with thy scenes,
  When worn by pain or overjoy,
Will leap the space that intervenes
  And roam thy wilds, once more a boy—
Imperishable beauty there,
Which wakes a love that knows not care.

IV.

The sun is up, and spreads his rays
  Of red and gold o'er earth and sky;
The air is full of sound; the ways
  Replete with early passers-by;
A city 'neath the horizon,
Breathes upward smoke of sallow dun.

A thousand thoughts of hate and fear,
  Of selfish interest, and of strife,

This ruddy radiance broad and clear
  Awakens into eager life;
The world's arena's torch is lit—
The weak to darkness must submit.

Millions, with flashing eyes of fire,
  Nerve for life's gladiatorial show,
That wave of blood which wafts us higher,
  Source of advancement and of woe;—
But two are deeply sleeping now,
With moonlight dew on each pale brow.

CANTO IV.

I.

A sound! The sound, the one sole sound
  All self-sustaining, echoless,—
Accompanying music spread around
  Time's slippered feet that onward press,—
Cadence of thought, all-languaged, free,—
The word's deep breathing—Hark! the sea!

Where the wind drives his viewless plough,
  And sows tempestuous seeds, and still
Sings as he sows—now deep-voiced, now
  In accents dissonant and shrill;
While flapping sails and sea-birds' wings
Keep concert as the giant sings.

A damp air, and a perfume salt
  From thousand flowers growing deep
In many a fretted, shelly vault
  Where breeze-like currents round them sweep,
And waft their fragrance fresh afar
Where'er the eternal waters are.

The ocean far before us spreads,
  Deep blue, with inlaid green and gray;
The sun begins to sink, and sheds
  A deepening lustre far away,
And where the rolling breakers come,
Flings fresh-cut roses 'midst the foam.

They roll as they have ever rolled,
  With sudden rush and quick return,
And with white, pointed fingers cold
  Plane the wet glistening sands; which burn
With a long, narrow, ruddy glare,
Though still the sun is high in air.

Above the waters' sidelong flow
  The sand spreads white, and deep, and dry;
The winds oft lift it up like snow,
  And bear it lightly whirling by,
Till wreath on wreath and drift on drift
It fills each new-indented rift:

For 'twixt the billows and the line
  Of hillocks low, whose grass is seen,
Half-buried, sparsely to incline
  Its sharp-edged blades of light cold green,
Are tracks of wheels and many feet,—
As men in crowds were wont to meet.

It is no wild and lonely coast—
  But here men build and congregate,
To see their little being lost
  Before the might they would abate;
For here alone assembled man
Can cast no shade on Nature's plan.

In twos and threes with listless eye
  Do many indolently stroll.

Lovers here whisper not—though high
  Their voices, they are in control
To the stern waves. Two brightly dressed
Come slow, apart from all the rest.

Can these be they whom last we saw,
  Creatures of moonlight and of shade,
Embodiments of Nature's law
  Wild beings by the moment made?
Can these be they? Around in space
The thought flies without resting-place.

Was it a mere fantastic dream,
  Born of the fevers of the mind,—
Some memory-freak, some sudden gleam,
  With poetry and midnight twined?
They look so like the unvaried crowd:—
But no—'tis they—And yet a cloud

Has dulled their features, and their feet
  Move heavily, as they would rest,—
Yet cannot bear those thoughts to meet
  Whose nearing flight is favored best
By stillness. What they may have been
Is lost in something dimly seen.

II.

They moved not with the careless bands,
  That still kept pacing to and fro;
With eyes upon the frothy sands,
  Their backs towards the western glow,
They wandered slowly ever on,
Till they are with the waves alone.

Then Helen lingered to behold
  The many-floated weeds—some brown,
Some tinged with amber, some with gold,—
  Oft on the beach a mass was thrown,
Which when the billow ceased to urge,
Divided the receding surge.

And once when at her feet was seen,
  As from an earthly garden come,
A broad bruised leaf of brightest green,
  She stooped to pluck it from the scum—
But memory checked her hand, and then,
Sighing she wandered on again.

Perchance she seemed a shade,—but no,
  The world has eyes which shame the lynx,
To scrutinize a woman (oh,
  How from its piercing stare she shrinks!)
'Twas a vain dream, for the world cast
No glance on Helen as she passed.

They stopped at last and gazed around.
  It was a turning of the shore,
The rounded outer point which crowned
  A long and gradual jutting; pour
The billows here more heavily,
The breeze comes fresher from the sea.

They marvelled they so far had come:
  To right and left along the coast

A white eternity of foam
  Gleamed on, and on, till sense was lost
In dreaming of beyonds beyond
The lines which sea and sky confound.

Red pulpy sea-weeds round were strewn
  And dark-ribbed shells; and near at hand
A wave-greened wreck peeped forth, which soon
  Must disappear beneath the sand,
As unprogressive souls sink down
Amidst life's cares wherever thrown.

A piece of drift here Edmond rolled
  To Helen's feet; they sat them down.
Her sun-lit hair flew uncontrolled,
  Now plaited by the winds, now blown
In massy strands across her face,
Hiding the sadness of its grace.

Her hand upon his shoulder fell
  As lightly as a flake of snow,
Within some silent wooded dell,
  And full as white; and slowly now
Beside her hand she laid her cheek,
And sighed a thought, but did not speak.

Her former proudly conscious mien,
  Her half-aggressive, playful air,
Were merged in a new softness seen
  Pervading all her being fair,
Like the sweet aspect of a flower,
Whose beauty is its only power.

Her eyes now followed Edmond's hand,
  Now tearful roamed across the sea,
While he upon the smooth white sand
  Carved figures strange; and on her knee
Resting the arm which held his head,
He chiefly thought, but partly said:

"So then our path of life has come
  To this lone point—and stops; for here
It merges in yon streak of foam:
  Our happy, glowing, fleeting year,
Since that bright August night has been
But preclude to this evening scene.

"No leaf-obstructed stellar ray
  Was e'er so thin as the slight thread
Which drags us from sweet life away
  And will not break—'tis doom unsaid,
'Tis man's opinion unexpressed,
Which draws us towards unwelcome rest.

"What is our fault? 'tis love—O hate,
  Revenge, and Envy, with lip curled,
And head erect, and eye elate,
  Ye boldly stalk the applauding world!
But love, and love in man alone,
No worth or beauty can atone.

"But now since nothing yet is known,
  And gazing in surrounding eyes,

No chilling shadow there is shown,
　A phantom future will arise,
And whisper, O return! this hath
But been a dream, pursue your path!

"Perchance 'twere stronger to return,
　And bear as much as flesh may bear—
No heroism here doth burn,
　There's nothing noble in despair—
But to behold you—no! Then fly!—
What means, what wealth for flight have I?

"The chase of knowledge and of art,
　The timely flight from conquering pain,
The power to obey the heart,
　Or o'er the mind's dominion reign,
Are magic grains which golden flails
Alone can thresh; naught else avails.

"That concentrate, conglomerate throng,
　That stone of which we are the grist,
The world so concrete, dense, and strong,
　Seems leaving us like blowing mist,—
As unto those in a balloon,
The earth seems sinking in a swoon.

"The world for us is like the bee,
　Which flies and leaves its sting behind—
Nay, 'tis a spectre suddenly
　Uprising on the passing wind,
And giving its decree of death—
Then melting like to frosty breath.

"We stretch our arms in eager prayer
    For mitigation or reprieve,
Adjuring but the empty air—
    And yet the fiat stern doth live;
Thus the world's heart is not of steel,
But air—O where should we appeal?

"To influence mankind's a thing
    For which long lives are but too brief,—
And we have moments—lingering,
    We would imagine some relief—
As if the tortoise Thought would speed
His steady foot for mortals' need.

"Yet here is comfort, in this state
    Of gathering and encroaching gloom,
The constant effort to be great,
    My early battle with the tomb,
The hope to serve my fellow-men,
Come sweeping brightly back again.

"How have I striven!—nay, still I strive!
    For though my form be in the past,
My thoughts, as I would hope, shall live—
    Ideas are in the present cast;
For written thoughts are living things
Which from Time's pinions pluck their wings.

"I would expound the toiling sage
    To hearts that of his theme would tire,

Condense the spirit of the age,
   And gift it with a tongue of fire—
Seeds would I scatter which shall bloom
When hands which sow are in the tomb.

"I fain would strike upon the bell
   Which mightier hands than mine have hung,
Till o'er the world one note should swell,
   One all-intelligible tongue—
The pæan of the mind set free,
And heart attuned to liberty.

"But 'words are wind'—yea, the wild winds
   That blow throughout thought's universe,
Whose unseen power nothing binds—
   Systems and empires they reverse;
Yet one may long these wild winds sow
Before the whirlwind 'gins to blow.

"My words are forth—but even without
   My humble momentary aid,
An autumn hangs above the sprout
   From which our bitter cup is made;—
But we may not evade the draught—
'Tis mixed, 'tis here, and must be quaffed."

His musings' stream why follow more?
   Its current and its course are seen.
Strange might it seem that on this shore,
   With ruin them and life between,
Edmond could thus control his brain
Unquelled, unparalyzed by pain.

Yet oh, remember that this thought
  Of doom was not then new, but long
Had been in all their feelings wrought;
  Their memories, too, a motley throng,
Kept back the vultures of despair,
Though close they hovered in the air.

That rainbow formed by human tears,
  Fair Hope, though faded, tinged their sky;—
Their beauty, strength, their youthful years,
  All daunted stern reality;—
The habit strong of living made
Death not a substance, but a shade.

III.

They saw the sun set red and round,
  With rayless disk and stifled beam;
A cloudy belt, by evening browned,
  A giant Saturn made him seem—
In vain he lingers there, for day
Hath passed him 'midst the vapors gray.

His rim had scarcely disappeared,
  When opposite his sinking place,
As broad, and round, and red, and bleared,
  The moon rose, with distorted face;
It seemed the sun beneath the sea
Had passed and risen suddenly.

As sank the smothered Western rays,
  And as the lightless moon arose,

They felt a creeping dull amaze,
  A lethargy without repose,
As far removed from sudden grief
As from the sigh of blessed relief.

A heavy hand seemed on them laid—
  They fain would rise, but could not try;
Though they had moved not, something made
  Them stiller seem, even to the eye—
For know there are two kinds of still,
One with, and one without a will.

The selvage of their thoughts was gone;
  These ravelled off in tangled shreds
Of ill-assorted colors wan—
  Faint fancies, memories, hopes, and dreads,
They fell unheeded one by one,
From the mind's fabric all undone.

Oft had they felt the same before;
  And anywhere but here, perchance,
A bird, a voice, an opening door,
  Had snapped this life-absorbing trance,
And given them time again to wait,
And ponder deeply o'er their fate.

But here, the unvaried sands around,
  The dim pall of the parted day,
But most, that deep, full, single sound,
  Kept outer influence at bay—
Why did they trust themselves alone
Beside that fatal monotone?

Death's coming steps where'er they fall,
  Upon the dull, sound-beaten coast,
Or echoing from the dungeon wall
  Of one whose hold on time is lost,
Cause but one feeling as they near,
A numbness scarcely mixed with fear.

The very lightness of his tread
  Pervades the ear and numbs the sense;
A helplessness to wake to dread,
  A dull absorption scarce suspense,
The fascination of despair,
Enwrap the mind and hold it there.

Unlike his sudden presence when,
  At moments when all hearts are glad,
He bursts into the sight of men,
  And drives them in an instant mad,
These footsteps faint of speed unknown
Turn all except the ear to stone.

IV.

The horses of their fate stood still—
  Their journey ended with the sands.
They showed no spirit, life, or will,
  While airy things with viewless hands
Unharnessed them; at close of day,
They led them silently away.

They dreamed no longer of return—
  The coursers of their fate were gone,

Led off by forms with faces stern.
  Behold them sitting there alone,
Beside the empty phantom wain
Their souls shall never mount again.

The red lights of the distant town
  Gleam in a faint and broken line;
The moon, now risen high, pours down
  Her bluish silver 'midst the brine,
And lights each sparkling flock of foam
That leaps from out its boundless home.

Upon the shore their shadows cling,
  And though the moon they must obey,
Who holds them there, stretch lingering
  Towards the far inviting ray,
As if they longed away to creep
From those two forms beside the deep.

And as they move, their shades draw near,
  And seem in eager whispering
To dwell upon some secret fear—
  To life can even a shadow cling?
They seem with wordless lips to say,
"Must we, too, follow in the spray?"

It might be but a whiter wave,
  Or moonbeam's more ethereal glance,
A heavier fall, or higher lave—
  A sudden something broke their trance,
And gave them power to feel and see
The deadly, near reality.

His features sharpened, and his face
  Grew waxen, while a troubled look
Crept 'neath its stillness—in his place
  He upright sat; but Helen shook,
And bent low with a shuddering moan—
Each felt, one instant, all alone.

Through her closed fingers oozed her tears,
  A crystalline, condensed despair,
Like the clear life-blood which appears
  On wounded flowers' stems; as Care
They gather slow on each pale hand,
Then dot with deeper gray the sand.

O essence of unmingled pain!
  O spirit of pure agony
Taking a woman's form! in vain
  Upon the sands thy salt tears lie—
So used the sands through endless years
To ocean's salter, painless tears.

How narrow, faint, o'ergrown with weeds,
  The paths of thoughts which lives control!
How humble, plain, and weak the reeds
  Which make the music of the soul!
The cold breeze on her wet hands dim
Called back her being all to him,

One thought absorbed her—he, her joy!—
  Upon her breast his head was strained—

"Oh waves, harm not my darling boy!"
    Convulsive, mingling kisses rained
Upon his forehead, lips, and eyes—
With each mad kiss a life-hope dies.

Oft had he striven to make her show
    The fulness of the love she bore—
He knew it, but ne'er saw till now,
    Upon this hope-abandoned shore—
Man ne'er receives a longed-for treasure
Till Time has ta'en its coffin's measure.

A look of triumph and of power,
    The old, old look of childish days,
Flashed forth in this extremest hour
    With sudden flare and torch-like blaze;
The moonlit smile his lips did wear,
Was drear, yet more than mortal fair.

And slowly down the beach they move,
    Locked in a clinging, warm embrace,
While with a look of speechless love
    She gazes up into his face—
Her life is in her eyes,—and they
Have not one glance for sea or spray.

Still down the shelving beach they glide
    Amidst wild wat'ry voices—hark!
The ever-beckoning ebbing tide,
    With its harsh whisper in the dark—
His gaze is far across the sea,
Perchance into Futurity.

They follow the receding wave,
  As if the ocean were their home,
Till now their waists the waters lave,
  And round them whirls the chilly foam;
But still her eyes are on his face,
Her soul's last, only resting-place.

A light cloud blurs the patient moon,—
  Patient from her eternity—
Their forms are water-mingled—soon
  They *must* appear—there! foam-wrapped, see
An object dark! 'twas but a wave—
How horribly the waters rave!

This cloud, oh, will it never pass!
  A human voice! or was't the ocean?
Ah, yes, yon moveless face of glass
  Glides forth with slow unhastened motion,
And lights the wind-indented plain—
The sea and sands for aye remain.

The play is o'er—the actors, where are they?
The world's vast theatre grows grim and gray.
No life seems near, save where a glimmer sheens
On the weird Hercules who shifts the scenes—
To Time I turn, with a bewildered eye,
And whisper to the spectre, *Plaudite!*

MESSALINA

A TRAGEDY IN FIVE ACTS

DRAMATIS PERSONÆ.

TIBERIUS CLAUDIUS DRUSUS CÆSAR,* fifth Emperor of Rome.
NARCISSUS, a freedman, secretary to Claudius.
PALLAS, comptroller of his household.
CALLISTUS, a freedman, favorite of the Emperor.
HALOTUS, his food-taster.
CAIUS SILIUS, a patrician, the consul-elect.
VESTIUS VALENS, a young noble, friend of Silius.
GETA, commander of the Prætorian guards.
VALERIA MESSALINA, wife of the Emperor, and also his cousin.
LEPIDA, her mother.
Soldiers, attendants, slaves, etc.

Scene, Rome, in the year 801 of the city (A.D. 48). The action occupies about eight days.

---

* There is collateral evidence that the upper part of Claudius's face was noble, but the lower part weak and exceedingly sensual. It is known, besides, that his appearance when at rest was majestic, but that when he moved about he was undignified and awkward.

MESSALINA

ACT I.

SCENE I.

A hall in the Imperial Palace.

NARCISSUS (*solus*).

So now I have a moment here alone.
It is not often that such moments come,—
In fact, so seldom that I am obliged
To shake myself to prove I am awake;
To pinch my mind, to prove that it is firm
And real and sound, and my own proper self,
And not half merged in the poor part I play.
It is a comfort, too, to talk out loud,
Myself unto myself, as I have done
From childhood; for it has a good effect,—
It gives consistency, resistance, force,
To my own inner life, which has to hold
Its own against the whirling life around,
Of which I make myself a constant part,
A part so perfect that I sometimes fear
My own identity is fading. But
It seems to thrive upon a food called hate
Which Contrast brings to me—a contrast strong—
That is, between myself, possessed of powers
Fitted to make some impress on our time,

Debarred from every noble aim, cut off
From every post of real dignity,
As much as the poor eunuch is from love;
And close beside me hundreds, languid, dull,
Debauched, depraved, inane, whom the law says
Are free competitors in honor's race.
What is the power I have, or may obtain?
It is to roll about for many feet
To trample on; and cringe, and cringe, and cringe;
And bow and bend; and whisper every word
That I would speak, and speak what I would roar;
And be the thing of one whom I despise—
That's dangerous!—and be his nothing, too,
If he so wills. There is no greater pain
Than a mind working, working day and night
Without a natural outlet. Evil is
In me no evil, hatred is not hate;
I cannot choose but hate the lives I feel
Legally crushing mine: and *how* I hate!
I wish this building would come toppling down
On me and all within it. I possess
At least a love to balance all this hate,
A love as strong, as real, and as true,—
The only one allowed me,—for myself.
A love unshared by aught in human shape—
No—yes—unshared? She is so mortal fair!
It makes me catch my breath to think of her.
If love and longing are the same, I love.
In any case, 'tis death or victory.
But then to win in such a case as this,
Where victory is so far, demands an eye
Of piercing gaze. It is a sorry sight
To see a mind well framed to govern men,

And rule with justice and discernment, driven
To find an outlet in most desperate schemes
To win a paltry woman. Let it be
Some comfort that she is her kind in one—
Passion's epitome—all sex condensed.
She wakes that love imbued with sex, which gives
Fire and force to those who have some aim
Worthy their higher powers; but on minds
Confined and cramped and driven within, like mine,
It acts as a corrosive, subtle poison.
Well, she shall never be my only aim;
For power is sweet, though won by self-contempt.
She is absorbed in Silius, that is plain;
It may be only fancy, but I hear
A something in her tone, when meant for him,
It never takes for others: but the look
She flashed on Valens, not two nights ago!
'Twas but a sidelong glance, but it contained,
Oh, what a knowledge, masterful, complete,
Intelligent, clear, boundless, of the world
Of Pleasure and of Passion, and of all
The troubling thoughts within their empire! Oh,
I would give years of life for such a look!
I shall not win it by remaining here.
I must keep near to Silius and to her,
And watch and wait, and still unravel slowly
The garment of their passion thread by thread,
To wear at last its tatters for my own.

                                        Exit.

SCENE II.

Enter VALENS.

VALENS.

I wonder what Narcissus, that dark bird
Of evil flight, sinister from his birth,
Was doing here. How I do wish that I
Had been a little closer—for I heard
(I'm sure of that) voices, conversing low,
And yet I only saw him flit away.
                    A female slave approaches hesitatingly.

By Hercules! come quickly, girl—'tis safe—
There's no one here—tell me at once your news.
Is it good or bad? my heart can wait no longer—
'Tis sick with waiting.

SLAVE.

                    It is wholly good,
If pleasure is a good, which is but pain.

VALENS.

How now, my young philosopher, you must
Have tried delight most carefully, to know
So much about it. I shall be well pleased
To try it with you when I can find time—
But let me have your news.

SLAVE.

You are to come,
When the moon sets, to the north postern, where
You will be met, and brought through winding ways,
In quiet and in safety, to the room
Where she who loves you will be waiting.

VALENS.

Oh,
This is too heavenly! I must be alone,
To think it over before it comes to pass,
And multiply my pleasure; and the mind
Should do the same with pleasure past, and dwell
Upon each tittle of our joy, until
Our life o'erflows with it.—Hark! what is that?
I thought I heard a step.—Yes, it draws near—
'Tis Silius! Hasten, fly!   *Exit slave.*

Enter SILIUS.

SILIUS.

Who is that slave
I saw you talking with? It seems to me
That I have seen her somewhere; is she not
A servant of the Empress?

VALENS.

You should know.
For my part, I cannot inform you.

SILIUS.

She
Seemed giving you some message.

VALENS.

                    You mistake:
'Twas I was trying hard to give to her
A message for herself alone—of love—
Good solid love, not too refined or thin,
Pouring it molten hot into her ears;
But she despised my begging blandishments,
And flouted me and fled.

SILIUS.

                    Ah,—was that it?
Tell me the latest news. You always are
The one to know it; thanks to your quick eye
Which misses nothing, and brings all things home
For your clear head to judge them.

VALENS.

                    Well, I own
The meshes of my mind are rather fine,
But catch more drift than fishes. The only news
I know of is that you are grown so large
The State looks somewhat smaller than before;
Or, if we use another metaphor,
I might remark that you have climbed so high
That one might think another in your place
Would feel a little dizziness or so.

SILIUS.

I have no power.

VALENS.

                    No, but you will have.
What use do you intend to make of it?

SILIUS.

I am not anxious to attain to it.
Power is an ugly peak, differing in this
From other heights, that it has no descent:
You must remain, or tumble headlong down;
You cannot climb down gently.

VALENS.

            If you fall,
Many in Rome will suffer. For my part,—
You know how I have loved you, and how long,—
But since that speech of yours which shook all Rome,
And even aroused the Senate from its sleep,
I feel a new and deeper admiration
For your great gifts. I have made up my mind
To stand or fall with you.
            But come, tell me,
Is it, then, true that she I dare not name
Not only fancies you, but loves you, too,
With her whole heart and soul; and giving up
All her past life, has vowed herself to you,
As purely, utterly, exclusively,
As any vestal to her sacred shrine?
Is all this true?

SILIUS.

        Why ask me, since you know
I cannot answer you?

VALENS.

        Why not, I pray?
You know her name has long been used by all
As common property.

SILIUS.

     More reason, then,
Why I should keep it sacred.

VALENS.

      But you know
She talks herself, from morning until night,
Of all she does—and it is much—and all
She thinks and feels, and, they say, all she *hopes*.

SILIUS.

You know that honor bears small tampering,
And least of all where women are concerned.
I made a rule, when first I donned the robe
Which made me man, never to break a trust
Reposed by any woman, be she queen,
Or slave, or public vendor of her charms.
You know I love you, Valens, and you know
'Tis not from any lack of confidence
I still keep silent.—Should an hour come
When you can aid me, may I hope to find
Your old support and friendship?

VALENS, *grasping his hand*.

       Yes, you may!

SILIUS.

Come, it is growing late. We will go back
To my house; and there have a little feast—
Nothing uproarious, but select and sound—
A few choice dancing girls, and some good wine

Undrugged with water, and some dishes framed
To be the gods of all the world of food.
What say you?

　　　　　　　VALENS, *constrainedly.*

　　　　　　　　No, I cannot come to-night.

　　　　　　　　SILIUS.

Why, what's the matter?

　　　　　　　　VALENS.

　　　　　　　　Nothing much, I have
Some business which will keep me very late.

　　　　　　　　SILIUS.

But it cannot be here.

　　　　　　　　VALENS.

　　　　　　　　Oh, no, not here;
Only I must go out by the back door,
It lies more in my way.

　　　　　　　　SILIUS.

　　　　　　　　It seems that you
Have taken up my lecture on the sex,
And put it into sudden practice, too.
I wish you all success. I hope that she
Is fair as your best dreams. Good-night!

　　　　　　　　　　Exit SILIUS.

VALENS.

Good-night!
If you but knew how fair, I think my chances
Were good to meet with Charon ere the dawn.
Within three hours I shall be there! It is
Too much—it stifles me to think of it.
            Glances around furtively and steals away.

SCENE III.

MESSALINA'S *apartment in the palace.* MESSALINA
discovered admiring herself in a polished mirror.
            Enter SILIUS.

MESSALINA.

I'd know that foot-fall 'midst a legion.—Ah!
            Sinks upon his breast, sighing.

SILIUS.

Oh, this is too delicious! such delight
Is almost pain: it seems so long—so long—
Since we last met: I can but gasp—each nerve
Was limp and dull and dead for want of you!
And now—they drink your touch. O heaven! I must
Be still, until my body can regain—
Some balance—   *A pause.*
            Even when thick folds of cloth
Divide our persons, it is still the same—
What matters it? for I am able still
To feel through mine the ripple of your blood,
And in your lightest touch to feel, know, see,

All we have ever felt before, endured,
Known, suffered, understood,—all gathered there,
Compressed, condensed, and then hurled forth, to flash
In one hot lightning thrill throughout my frame.

                    Drawing her down upon his knee.

When I am with you how the hours fly!
They are like Mercuries who scud along,
Running and flying with a following wind;
But when you are away, the hours lie cold,
Like gladiators dead, to be at last
Dragged off by Time. But why are you so still?
Do you not feel so?

MESSALINA.

                    Yes, and even more.
With us, in love and grief 'tis much the same—
Woman is silent if she greatly feels.
Her silence is herself, and she the strong,
Deep, living passion which awakes in man
Wild thoughts and words. She is the voiceless cloud
Through which the thunder rolls; or like the pine
Which lends the wind his music; or the vale,
Silent and still, which by its slope gives life,
Motion, speed, fury, to the bounding stream
Of man's loud passion; or she is the shore
Where man's desire rolls, and finds a voice.

SILIUS.

To break at last in foam,—foam scattered far,
Lost, unrecoverable; yes, of all
Your similes this last one is the best,
Because the end is nearest life's result.

Men ever try to fix what in itself
Is utterly unfixable, and strive
To press, mould, chisel to a lasting form,
An amorous woman, that swift-driving mist
And many-colored vapor.

MESSALINA.

Hush, for shame!
How can you speak so? when you know that I
Have lately begged of you to fix my heart—
Which needs no fixing—by a sacred tie
Checking the very possibility
Of change, making me yours beyond recall.

SILIUS.

You mean what we last spoke of?

MESSALINA.

Yes.

SILIUS.

You mean
A marriage solemnized in public?

MESSALINA.

Yes.

SILIUS.

It is a desperate venture.

MESSALINA.

Not at all.
All will declare for us, for you must see
That Rome is restless and dissatisfied.
You know this journey Claudius means to take
To Ostia; if he waver at the last,
I will contrive that he shall go,—and then,
Once wedded, Rome will be our own!

SILIUS.

You say
That all will join with us; but who are all?
What steps are taken? what is clear and sure?

MESSALINA.

No direct steps; but I have watched until
My instinct tells me that we cannot fail.
You know what Claudius is: a sage, an ape,
A mountebank, a just, an unjust judge,
An orator, an author and a fool,—
All pounded into one, yet mixed so ill
That each appears by turns, His clemency,
Always misplaced, and his severity,
Always ill-timed, have steadily divorced
Love from him upon all sides.

SILIUS.

That is true,
But has it flown to us?

MESSALINA.

You are so cold!

SILIUS.

I cold! But come, Valeria, tell me plainly
What you would do. I know that frequently
You have hinted at this marriage; now it seems
That you propose it to take place at once,
Instantly,—for you know that Cæsar leaves,
Or he may leave, within a day or two.
What are your plans? for you must have some plan.

MESSALINA.

My plan is a quick blow: 'tis twice as safe
As long-laid plots and complicated schemes,
Which fail and break in two half-way,
Frustrated in the working. I would call
Augurs and all our friends, and solemnize
A public marriage, with befitting pomp
And every outward circumstance; and when
We climb the steps (you know what steps I mean)
There's not a power in all official Rome
But will proclaim us sovereigns. As for *him,*
Dazzled and dazed, and losing heart at once,
As is his custom, he will suddenly
Take ship from Ostia; that will give us time
To fortify our power, appoint our friends
To all the highest offices, and send
Orders to take him when he lands.

SILIUS.

                              Your plan
Is a fine superstructure, but it seems
To lack that firm foundation which is found
To underlie successful plots.

MESSALINA, *starting.*

What's that!
Some one was moving then—I heard a noise;
Everything seems unsettled in the palace,
And I am nervous and unhinged to-night—
Let's talk of this to-morrow—no, to-morrow.
I cannot keep you longer, love: 'tis late,
And you must leave me.

SILIUS.

What, not now!

MESSALINA.

Yes, now.

SILIUS.

What is the matter?

MESSALINA, *confusedly.*

Why, —the Emperor—
He said he would not come, and now I learn
That he is coming—that he may arrive
At any moment.

SILIUS.

This is hard to bear.
I thought we had the night before us—well,
It must be borne—but it is horrible

To leave you thus, my thoughts in disarray,
My nerves unslaked, the fibres of my frame
In false relation.—When for many days
I am away from you, the impulses
Which are my springs of life grow weak and slow,
As the great nervous strength which you have given
Ebbs gradually away; and now I had
But just begun to feel some energy—
But this is vain! Come, give me, as I go,
Kisses for every step.

MESSALINA, *hesitating*.

Suppose I should
Send word to Claudius that I am not well,
Would you, then, love me more than ever, more
Than you believed you could?

SILIUS.

Hush, hush, be still.
You should not tempt me,—it might ruin us.
Good-night, my love. *Exit* SILIUS.

MESSALINA.

Good-night! Oh, how
I hate myself for this! Caius, come back!
But no, it is too late: I could not well
Stop Valens' coming if I wished; besides,
'Tis better to quite wear out pleasure's garments,
And then reclothe my heart for him I love.

SCENE IV.

MESSALINA'S *apartment.*

MESSALINA *is reclining voluptuously, while a female
slave timidly arranges her hair.*

MESSALINA.

You seem more skilful than you were last night;
It is a pleasure when you do it well,
It soothes and makes me drowsy.—Have a care!
You plucked a little then.—Stop shaking so!
I cannot feel you now; your touch has grown
Light and unpleasant, like a spider's web
Catching upon me.—No.—I need a stroke
Gentle and yet quite strong and firm—
Will you still hurt me me so? Take that, then!
> *Plucks a small dagger from her belt,
> and strikes her.*

SLAVE.

                                      Oh!
> *The slave-girl reels and falls fainting.*

MESSALINA, *turning away from her.*

Oh, agony of soul, to find myself
Tainted once more with crime! I'd gladly give
A province to undo this moment's work.
My love of pleasure has me by the throat,—
I am prepared to yield to it; but why
Must it drag other passions in, not mine,

And fling their weight upon my spirit, till,
Writhing in torment, it sinks whirling down,
Faster, yes, ever faster—

The slave moans.

The poor child!

I had forgotten her.

Strikes on a shield.

Attendants appear.

Take up this girl,
And do the very best for her you can.
She hurt herself; but 'tis not mortal.

Exeunt.

Yes,

I loathe this dread responsibility
Of living through no will except my own,
With no authority to fear yet love,
No hand to curb yet guide me.—Where could I
Find such an influence?—In Silius?
Perhaps; but no, there follows in his path
A gust of passion, and 'tis passion's breath
Has withered up my soul.—My mother, then?
That were a fairer hope; but then it is
Too late by far.—Yet it were sweet to try;
To sob myself asleep upon her breast,
And have her, with her cool and gentle hand,
Smooth all the fevered thoughts from out my brain—
Yet, this might be.

Enter attendant.

ATTENDANT.

The lady Lepida,
Your mother, waits without, and begs to know
If she may speak with you.

MESSALINA.

Well, did you say
That I was here?

ATTENDANT.

I did, my Empress.

MESSALINA.

You had no orders to. Could you not say
That you would see? If any one should come
While she is here,—you understand me.—Go,
Tell her to enter.

Exit attendant.

What unlucky chance
Has brought her here just now? just at the time
When Valens may arrive at any moment.

Enter LEPIDA *in a chair with four bearers. They set
down the chair, and* LEPIDA, *stepping from it, ad-
vances quickly towards her daughter.*

LEPIDA, *to the bearers*

Await without.

They take up the chair, and retire.

Valeria, my dear child,—
For you are still my child, whatever you do,
And dear to me, besides,—come, sit by me;
I will not tire you, so do not chafe.
I come because the spring of mother's love
Welling up in my heart o'erflows my lips,—
I cannot remain silent. Are you not
(It seems but yesterday) the self-same child
That used to nestle with your silky locks
Upon my heart, and bid me sing to you,
And yield obedience to my lightest wish

MESSALINA.

Obedience! that is not a pleasant word.

LEPIDA.

It is a sweet and gentle word, because
In giving up to me you only yield
To your own better nature. For you *have*
A fair side to your nature; and I come
To find the access to it, and to win
You back to be no longer what you are,
And to become what you were born to be.
Change for my sake, Valeria, change at once,—
It is much easier by a sudden break
Than to effect it inch by inch. I know
When you begin a settled life, it may
Seem dull at first; but in a little while
You will be glad, you'll thank me for it,—I
Promise you peace and perfect happiness.

MESSALINA.

Oh, pray do not begin to lecture me!

LEPIDA.

To lecture you! When I come here in love
And perfect gentleness, to win you back
By tears and prayers, when I could easily
Command you as your mother?

MESSALINA.

                And I, too,
Could as your empress—but I am, you know—
Order you to be silent.

LEPIDA.

               Just as well
Could you command your many sins and crimes
To hold their peace!—But why do you—for I
Will crush my anger back—why do you choose
To scorn me and my counsels and reproofs,
And lead a life so fraught to me with pain?

MESSALINA.

Because it is so pleasant.

LEPIDA.

             Oh, for shame!
To think that I should have produced a thing
To bring contempt forever on our house!

Messalina.

I wish that you would talk of something else,
Or come to me to-morrow.

Lepida.

                    Such a speech
Addressed to me! and when you know 'tis now
More than a month since last we met—O heaven!
Patience were now a crime! and mine is gone—
Now I will speak until, Valeria,
You hang your head in silence and in shame.
Why, not content with pleasures such as come
Within your reach (disgraceful in themselves,
But not quite patent to the world at large),
Wil you send forth your appetite, and make
All Rome your passion's garden, there to cull
Men even as flowers; and so make yourself
The property of those whom you despise,
And our old name a thing of scorn, till I
Would gladly tear it off, and trample it
Beneath my heel, deep in oblivion's dust,
If I could pluck it from me?

Messalina.

                    Since you have
Committed the imprudence to inquire,
I will reply and make my answer plain.
You know that all girls deem their mother pure,
Or are supposed to think so, and so I
Am doubtful, as I am in honor bound,
Whether in your own youthful, palmy days,
You had the self-same taste—well-poised and keen,

Discriminating, studiously formed—
For men that I have; but, for argument,
Let us suppose you had. Then you will know
That many men receive from Nature's hand
One gift in strange perfection, and a few
Are blessed with a great number; but not one
Has all endowments equally, and all
Perfect, without a flaw. I look abroad
And see one man who has a leg which makes
His spring like a bird's flight; another has
An arm like Hercules; and still a third
Has a grand torso, all in knotted welts
Of sculptured muscle. Here I see a man
Of god-like intellect, and then I meet
With one who is the exponent of the soul;
Another is but passion made alive,
Passion quick, frantic, tireless, and strong.
Now, if you will but grant me magic power,
Some wondrous alchemy, by which I may
Pluck his perfection from each one, and throw
These all into a crucible, and raise
One being from their ashes, who shall hold
Within himself those gifts which just before
Were parcelled 'mongst a thousand, but in him
Condensed, sublimed, commingled, ne'er to fade,
Then will I give myself to him alone,
Never to wander more.

LEPIDA.

                    Oh, monstrous thought!
Valeria, you have gone one step too far:
This insult is the last of many, and
It is the last you ever give to me.

My love has flown, far seeking, o'er your soul,
And, like a weary bird, comes back to me.
I go; and never more shall I return,
Till your proud heart lies supine in the dust,
Choking and bleeding, praying for my aid.
I now perceive that you are wholly lost;
And, since no other medicine will serve,
I here call down the vengeance of the gods,
And beg them hearken to a mother's curse!

MESSALINA.

No, no, not that!

LEPIDA.

It is too late; stand back!
May you be stripped (hear me, O gods!) of all
That now you have, and all that now you are,
And all you deem yourself, till naught is left;
Till you stand out a winter-blasted weed
In utter loneliness. May naught remain
Except confused regrets and memories wild,
And maddening thoughts of this your former life,
Which shall now beckon, now rebuff your mind,—
Shifting phantasmagoria weird and strange!
And when from out this awful chaos Death
Shall suddenly arise—the only form
Clearly defined—and shock your shrinking sight
With his cold visage and unmixed resolve,
Then may you feebly stretch your trembling hands
Towards virtue, as some comfort, if no shield,
And die at last in partial purity!

As MESSALINA *sinks upon a couch, covering her
face with her hands, the scene closes.*

ACT II.

SCENE I.

An inner room in the apartment of MESSALINA, *luxuriously and wastefully furnished.* MESSALINA *alone, lewdly attired.*

Enter VALENS.

MESSALINA, *without turning.*

A step so light proves some one here who comes
For no good purpose; I am half inclined
To seek the shelter of another room,
Without once looking round.

VALENS.

                By all the gods!
Do not do that!

MESSALINA.

Why? what has brought you here?

VALENS.

You know quite well.

MESSALINA.

No good motive, I fear,
Judging from your flushed cheeks and pouting lips
And half-drooped eyelids. Once again I ask,
What brings you here?

VALENS.

Pleasure.

MESSALINA.

And how do you know,
Why do you even think, that it is here?
You must have made some error.

VALENS.

Can I see
Pleasure before me, living, breathing, warm,
So potent, so condensed, so overcharged,
That my frame trembles, even at the sight,
And then not know her, though while I am speaking
I am convulsed with pain which yet is bliss?
Men may mistake their images for gods,
But hardly gods for images.

MESSALINA.

If I
Were not by nature so contained and cold,
Your words, which are but firebrands and coals
And bits of lighted tow—flung with a purpose—
Would have performed what you intend, and made
My blood take fire.

VALENS.

     Since you are so cold
And uninflammable, it cannot do
The slightest harm for me to sit down, thus,
Quite close beside you, and try to find out,
Most gently, if you are not meltable.
Now I will put a kiss between each pair
Of your dear fingers,—so. They will stand guard,
And keep your hands quite still while a vast host
Of other kisses, their sworn comrades, mount
To win your lips, and then from there sweep down,
Marching and countermarching o'er your neck;
If you will only let them. Now, I see,
Your cheeks are growing scarlet, and your eyes
Begin to have a light which puts out mine;
And then, to tell the truth, your upper lip
Begins to swell—indeed, 'tis puffed already—
They say that is a sign which never fails.
Now, when upon that lip I have imprinted
A few long, clinging kisses——

MESSALINA.

Rising and pretending to shake herself free.

     Stop, how dare you!
'Tis just three times that you have touched me: once
You kissed my hand, and once you jostled me,
In a thick crowd, and I did not exclaim;
And now you come unauthorized—and—and—
Why do you treat me so?

VALENS.

Because you are
Most beautiful. A beauty born to rouse
In human souls passion untamable,
And acting with that sure, resistless force
Of the great powers of Nature, as hot suns
Bring forth the leaves in Spring, or as the winds
Convulse the face of ocean.

MESSALINA.

Tell me, Vestius,
What would you have? would you prefer me coy,
Arch, winsome, timid, and yet almost bold,
Provoking dextrously your inclinations,
Fanning your fire with light, subtle strokes?
Or would you have me of a richer type,
Of temper more acknowledged, more robust,
A wilder, reckless passion?

VALENS.

I would have you
Exactly as you are to Silius.

MESSALINA.

Hold!
Breathe but his name again, we part forever,
And death shall follow you!

VALENS.

My Empress, pardon.

MESSALINA, *passionately.*

Tell me,—how would you have me?

VALENS.

As you are.

MESSALINA.

This, then, is as I am!

Throws herself into his arms.
Great Heaven! what's that?
'Tis steps—'tis he—hide, quick, or we are dead!

VALENS *hides himself behind the arras.*

SCENE II.

Enter SILIUS.

SILIUS.

Valeria, I have come.—Why, what's the matter?
Why are you dressed like this,—or undressed, rather?
Your face is half dissolved in pleasure, half
Stiffened with pain; your ears are scarlet, too,
And your cheeks white,—what is it?

MESSALINA.

I was ill
Before you left—I told you so—and still
I am oppressed by phantoms and strange fears.
I was just going to bed, hoping that there
I should forget them.

SILIUS.

                    What we spoke about
A little while ago inflamed my mind
To such a point I could not think of sleep.
I could not even quit the palace. But
I stayed where I could glance from time to time
Through the grand entrance, so as to be certain
If Claudius came here. Since you saw me leave
Your outer door, I have paced steadily,
Without once stopping, the long corridor,
And thinking, thinking till my brain became
Breathless and faint. I knew the time had come
To take a quick decision, yes, or no,
And then to act; and I am here to say
That I, at last, have quite made up my mind—
All doubt is over, action has arrived—
I am resolved to——

MESSALINA.

                    Stop! say nothing more.
Tell me some other time—not now!

SILIUS.

                              But why?
Do not you wish to hear?

MESSALINA.

                    No, wait!

SILIUS.

                              But why?

MESSALINA.

The time is not auspicious. I am sure
If you speak now you will regret it.

SILIUS.

Ah!

MESSALINA.

What makes you start so?

SILIUS.

I heard something move,
Or something breathe, I can't tell which. It seemed
To come from near that screen; I'll go and see.

MESSALINA.

Stand still, in heaven's name! Don't look behind it—
It is a deadly omen! If there were
Anything there, my own prophetic sense
Would tell me, and I then should say to you,
Go quick, at any risk!—Help, I am faint.

SILIUS.

Turning towards her.

What is it,—are you dizzy, darling?

VALENS *slips away.*

MESSALINA.

Oh!
A pause.

I feel a little better, love. Then was
Some dark prophetic entity, some thing
Of evil omen, creeping near our lives,
And threatening to invade their circle; for
I felt its icy breath,—but now 'tis gone,
And we can live and hope. What happiness,
To enter into life again! Come, love,
Sit close beside me, tell me everything.
What are your plans, what do you mean to do?

SILIUS.

Why are you grown so humble suddenly?
It is not like you; and above all now,
When my plans, as you call them, are but yours.
At any rate I have made up my mind
To act as you propose, and quickly too;
But we must take some order; it is folly
To leave so much to chance. Remember, though,
If ruin follow, as seems probable,
That the world's empire was far less my prize
Than you, Valeria. Now to business. Will
You give me leave to speak to Valens? He
Hinted at this affair not long ago,
But, as I had not your authority,
I put him off. Shall I make sure of him?

MESSALINA.

Who, Valens, did you say? Yes, I suppose so.

SILIUS.

How unstable you are, Valeria!
I know that you know Valens well, and now,

Upon some whim, some lethargy of mind,
You scarce recall him. If we mean to win
We must be practical about this matter.
We must have every detail of our scheme,
Mad though it may be, clearly understood,
And each agreed upon. Now to begin:
You know we cannot move a single step
With the Prætorian troops against us; but
If Geta, their commander, could be won!

Messalina.

You have some influence with him.

Silius.

                    I have,
And I will try my best to win him over.
I don't despair of him; but there is one
Stronger than Geta, one who, like the mole,
Working in dirt and darkness, raises all
The mountains of our cracking Roman world.
Petty court politics are now our world;
We call them mountains, they are mole-hills still.

Messalina.

Hush, not so loud. You mean Narcissus.

Silius.

                          Yes.

Messalina.

He is the power that moves the Emperor.

SILIUS.

We cannot do without him, possibly.
You know him best, and can approach him safest.
Choose your time well, and offer anything.
I need not school you in diplomacy,—
But stick at nothing, so that we may have him.
Will you accept the task?

MESSALINA.

          I will. But hear me:
You say sometimes I am too silent, now
I long to speak to you. You told me, love,
In the same breath that you believed my plan
Was but another name for ruin. Yes,
You know you meant that; but in the same breath
You said that you adopted it, and there
You showed me virtues, vigors of the soul
Beyond my daily vision. Why, oh why
Is my sight so confined, so fixed upon
Life's foreground? But a change has come.
I feel that through the rite about to be
I am already wholly, proudly yours,—
Yours, and yours only.

SILIUS.

         Why more fully mine
Now than before? My own dear love, you know
You were and are all mine, and I all yours.

MESSALINA.

It is the weakness of a woman's heart
To live through forms. I cannot alter it;

And since to women I must still be kin,
I am determined to surpass them all
In desperate earnestness. You see this vase!
It is a fitting type of my past life,—
Too rich in ornament, too poor in strength.

Dashes down the vase.

Where is it now? gone, and my past with it!
Shattered to fragments, quite forgotten, dead!
From this day forth, I swear to be to you
Your empress, leman, friend, companion, slave,
Aught, anything you will!—the lamp which burns
Only to light your way; the voice which sounds
Only to soothe your ear, the heart which beats
For you alone. Caius, receive my troth!

Kneels.

Take with it all I have, am, may become,
My fixed fidelity, my soul itself!

ACT III.

SCENE I.

An audience chamber in the palace.

CLAUDIUS *partially reclining.* MESSALINA, NARCISSUS, *and attendants grouped about him.*

CLAUDIUS.

This is an absurd story, by Augustus!
I can't imagine what gave rise to it—
This rumor which has spread abroad that I
Was spattered by the blood of a flamingo
At sacrifice. No evil omens come
Near me. My wife is far too fair for that;
Her beauty is a living augury,
A happy and a constant omen. No,
The gods were friendly to me from my birth;
For they resolved to give me the whole world
When I was nothing but a wretched outcast,
A wind-blown speck, the merest accident
Lost in Caligula's rough reign. And then,
Not satisfied, they added to the gift
The fairest woman in all Rome, the queen
Of love and pleasure; but, as I was saying,
It never came into my mind that I
Should be an emperor; but, for all that,
I have made a good one. Some have called me cruel,

And fond of blood. I wish I had them here!
I'd beat them, by Augustus, with thick chains!
Have they so soon forgotten my mild nephew,
Gentle Caligula? That was a reign!
Let them remember it, and then compare
His rule with mine, and they will have to own
That mine resembles Numa's reign beside it.
It is all gentleness and perfect peace.
Is that not true, Narcissus?

NARCISSUS.

　　　　　　　　　　Noble Cæsar,
It is quite true, but rather understated.
You are a bright example to be followed,
A living proof that Justice need not frown,
But may wear Mercy's smile. You are, in fact,
A monument of gentleness. You stand
Wrapt in that clemency which comes from strength.
But for the peace you spoke of, I must own
I do not see as much in your great reign
As your pure heart deserves; we do not have
All that we ought to have.

CLAUDIUS.

　　　　　　　What is it you mean?

MESSALINA.

He merely means that the affairs of state,
Perpetual over-straining for your good,
Have vexed and wearied him.

NARCISSUS.

          Cæsar, I mean
That rumors reach me of unsettlement
In many people's minds, who ought to be
Contented. It is whispered that there are
          Glancing at MESSALINA.
Some who are great who would be greater still,
And even try——

CLAUDIUS.

        You do not mean to say
That there is hidden danger?

NARCISSUS.

          I can scarcely
Tell what to think.

MESSALINA, *significantly*.

        Narcissus is a man
Of such pure heart and such devotion to
Our welfare, that if I could find some way
To still his mind's uneasiness, no matter
At what a cost, at what a sacrifice,
He might command me.

NARCISSUS.

        I have but one love,
One reverence alone which equals that
I feel for Messalina. It may be
That I was over-anxious.

MESSALINA.

It is certain.

CLAUDIUS.

Come here, Valeria—there—no, closer still.
            Takes her upon his knee.

Now give me that kiss you are mistress of.
                        She kisses him.
No woman in all Rome can kiss like that!
How did you ever learn it? By Augustus,
It makes me dizzy! You can make your lips
Cling as no other can, and, then, the instant
I take my lips away, you kiss me.—Ah!
The memory of it now makes me feel faint.
                        A pause.

I am inclined to give up the whole project,—
This trip to Ostia. Why should I go there?
I thought I took an interest in the matter,
That monstrous dike and harbor I am building;
But, after all, what is the use of it?
The sea some day will roll there unopposed,—
It will be all forgotten. I suppose
You could not leave Rome with me?

MESSALINA.

                        Cæsar, no.
That is beyond my power. I have now
A thousand things to keep me here. Each one
Taken alone is slight, but as a whole
They are despotic. I shall miss you greatly,—

You know how hard it is to let you go.
But then I love your fame as much as you;
You will return with all your plans perfected,
And the work well begun which is to be
Your greatest monument. 'Tis not the same
To leave such work to others,—this is yours,—
Yours and yours only; and when you return,
Proud of your triumph, I will be proud, too,
And come to welcome you.

CLAUDIUS.

                    I cannot tell.
What do you think, Narcissus?

NARCISSUS.

                    It was planned
That we should start at once; but suddenly
I thought I saw some reasons which should make us
Incline to stay. And yet I think some reasons,
Weightier, perhaps, should make us go. Indeed,
We ought to take some hours to think it over.

CLAUDIUS.

You are a living cunning! Luckily,
Most of it is in my behalf. But then
You know they do say that if you and Pallas
Would only take me into partnership,
The treasury would be full. There, do not look
So cheap and foolish; it is human nature—
A vile one. I believe that I will go
To Ostia; and a bright idea has struck me:
I mean to have a little sliding table

Rigged in my carriage; so that as we drive
We two can play, and so, with luck, perhaps
I may win back some tithe of what is mine.
I think to-morrow we might start; but now
My time has come for study,—I must go.

CLAUDIUS *rises to pass out.*

MESSALINA.

In an undertone to NARCISSUS, *as she passes him.*
Meet me to-night, at midnight, in the room
In front of my own chambers. I will see
That all the guards are absent.

NARCISSUS.

I will come.

Exeunt.

SCENE II.

An alcove of the temple of Mars.

Enter GETA, *meeting* PALLAS.

GETA.

Well met, Pallas, I'm glad to see you. Have
You seen Callistus?

PALLAS.

Yes, I saw him.

GETA.

Where?

PALLAS.

Quite near here. He'll be here in a moment.
He was pretending to be drunk, and making
As if he would go elsewhere, and slouched on
This way by simple chance.

GETA.

                    That was just like him!
He is too shrewd for us,—if you can call
Low cunning shrewdness. I have never seen
Any one man who would take so much trouble
To act out a deception, even where
The advantage is invisible! I tell you,
A man like that is hard to treat with; for
While your whole mind is bent on gaining over
A convert to your views, his mind is fixed
On gaining gain.

PALLAS.

He's brave, at any rate.

GETA.

He may be brave.

PALLAS.

I see you do not like him.

GETA.

Oh, yes, I like him well enough; but then
With such a man——

PALLAS.

Hush! he is coming in.
Enter CALLISTUS.

GETA.

Callistus, I am very glad to see you,—
Sincerely glad. It seems a proper time
For us, who are all members of one household,
To learn each other's views. Where is Halotus?

CALLISTUS.

We started out together, but of course
We separated. Still, he said at parting
He would be here before me. I suppose
He stopped for some strong wine; for he complained
That he felt faint, from tasting endless foods.

Enter HALOTUS.

HALOTUS.

I wish I had the man who first invented
This curse of food! I'd beat him long and lightly,
So as to hold the life in him until
He should feel himself die. My life has been
Poisoned with food! My health is wrecked. Besides,
I can't enjoy a single honest meal;
For everything I try to eat suggests
Some culinary horror.

GETA.

Well, have patience,
You may have vengeance yet. Friends, it would be

Folly for me to make a speech to you.
This meeting is entirely informal.
I only thought that if there should be trouble
(And it seems probable), by meeting here,
Quietly, in this way, we should be able
To act in concert. I feel for you all
A real affection, and my only wish
Is that we all may safely float together
Upon the next high tide. You know there are
Strange rumors, and strange thoughts and new ideas;
Confusion is beneath the court's smooth surface.
What will the issue be?

CALLISTUS.

              To tell the truth,
I have not one idea about the matter.
My mind is vacant. You must tell me more
Before I can begin to think.

PALLAS.

              What rumors
Are those you spoke of,—the new thoughts you said
Were gaining ground?

GETA.

              Oh, nothing positive.
You know the Emperor at sacrifice
Was spattered with the blood of a flamingo.
Some say it means a change of sovereignty.

CALLISTUS.

But what do you say? We will trust to you.

GETA.

I am not skilled in omens. Come, Halotus,
You have not spoken yet, tell us, in terms
Which are not doubtful, what you mean to do
Amidst these changes.

HALOTUS.

    I will tell you plainly.
I mean to wait, and wait until I know
Which side will win, and then to take that side,
And be well paid for my fidelity.

GETA.

That's it! They say that for all those who side
With the new party, there will be a rain
Of sesterces,—at least for those who hold
Their aprons out in time.

CALLISTUS.

    But some contend
It will rain heads instead.

PALLAS, *to* CALLISTUS.

    We shall arrive
At nothing in this way. Let us suppose
That there should be a struggle presently,
Between the party dominant at court
And a new party led by a great Roman,
A powerful patrician, on whose side
Would you be found?

CALLISTUS.

             I cannot well believe
That there will be an actual convulsion,
A struggle for supreme control.

GETA.

                    They say
That Silius is the strongest man in Rome,
And growing stronger.

CALLISTUS.

                 Silius is strong.
But he is much too good a man to try
To wreck the State. Besides, since we are now
Upon that subject, I will tell you plainly
Silius has hurt himself by his good deeds
More than by all his bad ones. His new law
Against suborned informers and all those
False advocates who help the wrong for bribes,
And prostitute their talents, has but made him
A host of foes. He has a healthy mind
And healthy heart; and in a poisoned air,
Like this of Rome, such natures are the first
To be struck down. The only men who thrive
Are those who, like ourselves, are morally
A trifle tainted.

PALLAS.

             It is time to go.
There must be some agreement. If the troubles
Which Geta fears should suddenly arise,

Shall we all stand together, and be found
On the same side?

CALLISTUS.

I hope so, I am sure;
In fact, I know so. I am confident
There is not one of us who will not try
To help the cause of right, stability,
And justice. You know Justice has one face,
And only one,—not two, like Janus. Yes,
I feel we four shall act as one.

GETA.

Callistus,
I thank you from my heart. Good-by!

CALLISTUS.

Good-by!

PALLAS, *in an undertone to* GETA.

When the strain comes, I'll pull with you.

GETA, *as they go out.*

The strain
Will come; it is beginning now.

CALLISTUS.

*Who has pretended to go out in an opposite direction;
but who has only hidden behind a column, dragging
HALOTUS after him.*

Halotus,

Do not be influenced by a single word
That man has spoken, or you will be lost.
It is just possible we may be able
To get an order from the Emperor
Putting a safe man in this Geta's place.
I am not sure,—if not, it means our ruin.

Exeunt.

SCENE III.

*The Palatine hill. Midnight. The city visible below
in the moonlight.*

*Enter SILIUS alone; he pauses, and leans against the
rampart.*

SILIUS.

So Geta promises that he will join us;
That gives our cause new strength. But, as he says,
This should have been determined long ago.
How have the days slipped by! Days? weeks and
months,
All spent in pleasure, utterly consumed,
Which should have been devoted to the winning
Of the whole court,—canvassing every man,—
Making so sure that stepping on the throne
Would scarcely have produced a jar. But then
They were delicious days! O heaven, the scenes
That we have known! But they have left us here
With an uncertain fate. It is Valeria

Who keeps our future doubtful, and our lives
Forever in the balance; for her mind
Is woman's mind in its entirety.
She always thinks just what she wants to think.
She would enjoy the empire all at once
In her own way. She cannot bear to wait
To arrange each detail, and so to assure
Possession. She believes it is enough
That Claudius has a flaccid grasp of power,
To make it safe for us to disregard
All rules of prudence, and to suddenly
Seize the whole empire, as a fitting home
To love and revel in. It seems to her
That he must sink with his own weight; and, then,
That all men, seeing us upon the throne,
And that we grace our station, will agree
To do us homage. I am growing like her.
There's no escape from that, for she is mine,—
She loves me and has often proved it. I
Have grown to be a portion of her life.
I still have my own separate, stronger thoughts,
But they flit by me like some moving dream.
I feel my virtue slipping from my soul,
And yet I know not how, nor when, nor where,
As heat and cold and wet and dry depart
Before the ever-changing winds. 'Tis strange
That if she were of a chaste, even temper,
Serenely passionate, I should not need
To have her so forever in my thoughts.
But as it is, her life alone seems real.
I see the moving whirl of eager Rome;
The gatherings of men; the plots, the troubles
Which now surround us. I see our own peril,

And even the remedies. But it all seems
Something ill-timed, unnatural, out of place,
Not quite an ancient tale, yet more remote
Than Messalina's life,—my life with her,—
Where everything, from first to last, contains
A present reason and a living charm.

The world, made mystic, and so purified,
By the blue moonlight, stretches at my feet,—
For Rome is now the world. How beautiful
This glimmering scene of palaces and temples,
Pile upon pile, rising mysteriously
From the black shadows! This whole sleeping world
Is waiting for a ruler. Antony
Lost this same world for one weak woman's love,—
And Silius,—no, that is not history yet.
The chances are still strongly on our side.
In fact, they never were so strong; for now
Geta has given his promise, and with him
And the Prætorians, we can hardly fail.
A something tells me we are sure to win,—
Hail to the omen!—and to prove it true
I will awake, and put forth every power
To win, not lose, the whole world for a woman!

Exit.

Enter NARCISSUS, *moving stealthily along the*
parapet.

NARCISSUS.

I wish I knew what Silius was saying.
He thought himself alone, and so spoke out,—
At least I think so, for I could not hear

Another voice with his. I almost caught
The words. At any rate, I saw his face,
And its expression said as plain as words
That something desperate is afoot. I fear
This Silius; he has too much on his side.
It is just possible he may be able
To overwhelm us all in general ruin.
I have one great advantage, though: this crisis
For me is furnished with a double exit
On the safe side; for I can try to win
By hurling down, or holding up, the State.
To-night decides which effort it shall be.
It is a desperate venture! for things desperate
Are not the times of strife and clashing swords,
But of suspense between alternatives;
Those quiet, anxious moments whose decision
Directs the swords, and tells them where to plunge.
Why do I stand and reason with myself,
And loiter, and delay, and try to hope
That somehow, all at once it will grow easier
To face this interview? I have so longed
For such a chance, even when it seemed beyond
The range of possibility; and now—
I shall be braver when the moment comes—
But now my nerves are utterly unstrung.

                                        Exit.

SCENE IV.

The outer room of the apartment of MESSALINA.
  MESSALINA *reclining upon a couch of skins, and lost
  in thought.*

        NARCISSUS *enters stealthily.*

MESSALINA.

What is the night, Narcissus?

NARCISSUS.

                              It is clear.
The moon is shining on the sleeping city,
Which *looks* most peaceful. You, perhaps, can tell
Whether it is so; for, as empress, you
Have the best means of knowing.

MESSALINA.

                           As you came,
Did you meet any one upon the way?

NARCISSUS.

I thought I saw—I may have been mistaken—
Our consul just elected.

MESSALINA.

                    Silius? Where?

NARCISSUS.

Not far from here upon the Palatine.
I gathered from a look I seemed to see
Upon his face, that he was meditating
Some great move in life's game. And then it came
Into my mind that I, perhaps, was summoned
In this connection, for some information,
Or some slight aid I might be able to give
To a great undertaking, and, of course,
A good one.

MESSALINA.

You are wrong, as often happens
With minds too keen. For, as for Silius,
I think he is too much in love with me
(If you will pardon me) to do or think
A single thing which does not bear upon
The keeping and increasing my affection.

NARCISSUS.

Then why have I been summoned?

MESSALINA.

I cannot
Admit I summoned you; or if I did,
It was because I've noticed for some time
A something in your manner and your look,
Which seemed to say that you were on the watch,
Waiting and hoping for a chance to speak.

NARCISSUS.

Well, if I was not summoned, I suppose
I may as well depart. Good-night, my Empress.

MESSALINA, *agitated.*

Since you are here, I think it would be best
To stay a moment. You know, for myself,—
Myself alone,—that I am fond of power,
And apt to long, in a vague, aimless way,
For what I have not, and it might occur
That you could aid me.

NARCISSUS.

   This is waste of time!—
Time which is precious. We shall never gain
One inch of ground by sparring,—it is hopeless,—
We are too closely matched. You see me here
Firmly convinced that you have need of me
For some great purpose,—what, I do not know,
And do not wish to know; but I am ready
To give my fullest aid.

MESSALINA.

   On what conditions?

NARCISSUS.

I was the first to take the risk, and lay
My thoughts before you; now, it seems that you,
As being the stronger, should first state to me
Your portion of the terms.

MESSALINA.

   The terms are these:
You must remain in utter ignorance
Whether I have a plan, or not; and I—
Should a design to gain more power exist—
Would give my word to tell you all in time
For you to act with vigor and success.
But you must swear to give your utmost aid,
No matter what I may demand.

NARCISSUS.

These terms
Are very hard,—harder than I expected.
And yet I think I could accept them—if—
What shall be my reward?

MESSALINA.

More power, by far,
More wealth than you have now, a thousand times.

NARCISSUS.

These are great things; but I have more of both
Than I deserve. I do not long for more.

MESSALINA.

Have you no overpowering wish, then?

NARCISSUS.

Yes.

MESSALINA.

What is it? Speak!

NARCISSUS.

I dare not.

MESSALINA.

Do not fear
To name your wish, and state your own conditions,
Just as I stated mine.

NARCISSUS.

If I could hope
That I am not now so repulsive to you
As I once was——

MESSALINA.

I do not understand.

NARCISSUS.

Have I your promise that in no event—
No matter what I wish, or hope, or ask—
You will be scornful, or will feel resentment,
And follow me with hatred?

MESSALINA.

Yes, I promise.

NARCISSUS.

Then let me say at once that I believe
That all that you desire might be placed
Within your reach.

MESSALINA, *aside.*

Awful temptation! How?

NARCISSUS.

It is the telling how demands your promise.

MESSALINA.

You have it,—speak!

NARCISSUS.

                    You know I love you—yes,
You know it perfectly.—Give me the tithe
Of the love which you waste on those who are
Beneath your very notice! I adore you!
Give me yourself, just as you are,—all stained,
Soiled by the world, and yet sublime in beauty!
And I will make your will the supreme law
Of all the world. Why are you silent?

MESSALINA.

                                        Oh,
This situation is an agony!
I see success within my easy reach,—
I may have all I wish for, and long years
To fill with it,—love, pleasure, power,—and yet
In payment, I must make myself unfit
To enjoy one hour.

NARCISSUS.

                    You cannot pretend
That you despise me so, since you could stoop
Even down to Mnester, that low-born comedian.

MESSALINA.

For once, your wit has failed you; to accuse
A woman is the best means that I know
To make her prove herself quite chaste to you.
Your charge is mean and false! Let us break off
This interview at once. You have my answer,—
I dare you do your worst!

NARCISSUS.

          My worst might be
A little troublesome,—a trifle dangerous;
For instance, I might choose to make a hole
In the court screens,—a little one, you know,—
Just big enough to let a ray of daylight
Fall on the death of Appius Silanus.

MESSALINA.

You might as well attempt to tame a lion
With a light switch, as to tame me by *fear*.
I dare you do your worst!

NARCISSUS.

            Hear me, Valeria!
I love you so that I could never harm you;
I would not injure you by word or deed.
Love me a little, even with contempt,—
Give me the waste, the skimmings of your love,—
And I will pledge my life that I will carry
Not only you, but those you hold most dear
Up to the very highest pitch of power.
You hesitate,—O Heaven! that means consent!
I see you yield, I feel that you are mine!
I would die beaten into shreds with chains
For this one moment! Oh, at last!
                He embraces her.

MESSALINA.

                Away!
Oh, let me go! You're killing me with shame!
            Shaking herself free.

Your slavish touch has coursed through my whole
    frame
With a long thrill of horror.—I am changed!
The blood of all the Cæsars in my veins
Boils up, and tells me how I have betrayed
The life that I was born to, and have stooped
To herd with things even as base as you,—
But I can rise, and that you never can.—
Back to the lower regions of the world,
The life where you belong, the slums, the purlieus!
This is a purer air than you can breathe,
And it is poison to you!

NARCISSUS.

            Hear me, though!
Listen this once! Listen,—it is too late,—
You are pledged to me, and cannot now draw back.
    *He attempts to embrace her again, following
    her as she retreats before him.*

MESSALINA, *drawing a dagger*.

A scratch from this is death,—and if you touch me,
I shall strike quick and deep. For here I stake
My soul's new purity against your life!
Away! your life's in danger!
                 Exit NARCISSUS.

  She lets fall her dagger, and sinks upon the couch.
                 Oh, my love!
I fear that this, my first fidelity,
Will cost us more than all my former treasons.

ACT IV.

SCENE I.

The road to Ostia.

Enter CLAUDIUS *in a chariot, playing at dice with*
NARCISSUS; *and accompanied by* PALLAS *and a*
numerous retinue.

CLAUDIUS.

Stop the coach here! this scenery is attractive.
I will get out and stretch myself. Besides,
I've won enough,—enough, at any rate,
To keep you busy digging, for a while,
Into the treasury, before you can
Repay it.

> *Descends, with* NARCISSUS *and* PALLAS, *from*
> *the coach, which drives on slowly.*

NARCISSUS.

Cæsar, you have wondrous luck!
It never fails. You hold it from the gods.

CLAUDIUS.

I know you think I cheat; but I do not.
Yet if I did, it would be only fair
To make you give a little something back

Out of the enormous sums you take from me.
Yours is a bigger game than mine. It is
More risky, too. Your dice are human lives,
And the stake Rome.—Well, it amounts to that.
Cheating, you know, is the life of your game;
And you play fairly well. But, then, some day
You'll lose a throw,—one throw would, in your case,
Be quite sufficient,—and the forfeit is
Proportioned to the greatness of the game.

> *Enter a messenger.* Narcissus *and the messenger whisper apart.*

> Claudius *turns to* Pallas.

I'm hungry, Pallas; so I hope you have
A good full banquet ready. Where's the place?

PALLAS.

I ordered all prepared that I could think of,
And the meal spread beneath a clump of elms
Upon the road-side, half a mile from here.
I did not know that you would leave your carriage.

CLAUDIUS.

That can be managed.

> *Turning to* Narcissus.
> Well, what does he say?

NARCISSUS.

Cæsar, the messenger has little news.

CLAUDIUS.

I asked you what he said.

NARCISSUS.

'Twas chiefly this,
That Lucius Pollio died last night near Rome.
He died in his own bath, under the care
Of a physician.

CLAUDIUS.

Then, that means that you
Caused this man's death. And why? What harm
    had he
Committed against you?

NARCISSUS.

No harm to me,
But harm against the State. I feared the man;
For though he had done nothing overt yet,
He had a reckless and unsettled mind.
His friends were so debauched, and all his courses
So wild, and even impious, that we all
Thought him a dangerous man.

CLAUDIUS.

And do you call
This news of slight importance, that in Rome,
Here in my home, in my own capital,
Under my very eyes, a Roman noble,
A man of consular degree and rank,
Is killed without my orders? Do you mean
To make my city, my imperial Rome,
A dark and foul and dingy cell, where death

Creeps none know whither? Where gray, grisly
    forms,
Monsters of ruin, dimly crawl about
As you direct them?

NARCISSUS, kneeling.

     Mercy, Cæsar, mercy!
Spare those who acted from the noblest wish,—
The wish to strengthen your great, glorious house,
And to preserve your god-like self, that staff
On which we all must lean.

CLAUDIUS.

     To one who looks
Upon this matter with the quick hot glance
Belonging to a natural man,—a man
Untutored and untrained, and much impressed
By first appearances,—this murderous deed
Seems horrible; but to philosophy

NARCISSUS sighs and rises.

It is not so. For when a man is dead,
Philosophy, deny her as we may,
Will whisper he deserved it. As for him,
This Pollio, I cannot regret him much.
It is one man the less, at any rate;
That is a comfort.

     Now, in your own case,
Let us suppose that I had condemned you
To the same fate,—now looking at it fairly,—
Would you not have to own that you deserved it,

That the idea was happy? As for me,
I know I merit death—well, every day;
But there are forms which, rising out of life,—
Expressing by their beauty all its dreams
Scattered through centuries,—were not intended
To fade away and die. Valeria, now,
Was never meant to die, and leave the world
Without one model, concentrate and full,
Of woman's charm. I think I will return.
She has a witchery beyond all thought,
And then such glorious limbs! It is a waste
Of our one single life, this making harbors
And building dikes, with Messalina near,
In easy reach. I feel the need of her,—
I will go back.

NARCISSUS.

Cæsar, I beg of you
That, as you value your own peace and safety,
You will continue on your way to Ostia!
I cannot tell you what is happening yet,—
I do not know precisely,—but from spies
I learn that Rome is on the very verge
Of outbreak. There's a plot,—'tis in the air,—
It will burst forth.—But from this vantage-ground
You cannot fail to master it; and then
You will return in triumph.

CLAUDIUS.

If there is
The slightest danger in returning now,
I would not think of it. Let us go on.

I wish you had not told me there was danger,—
You have half spoiled my hunger. Tell them there
To bring me a led horse. At any rate,
I'll try the quality of Pallas' banquet.

               Exit, with his soldiers and attendants.

NARCISSUS, *shaking his hand towards Rome.*

Lady, take care! The empire is here!
I have it with me, and shall keep it, too;
It may return and crush you. Ah, take care!

                          Exit.

SCENE II.

The gardens of LUCULLUS.

At the back of the scene MESSALINA *has caused an archway to be constructed, so contrived that no one can look behind it, and that from the front it gives the impression of looking through it upon the sea-beach and the ocean beyond. Sea-nymphs are clustered here in waiting.*

Near the centre of the scene there is an altar with a fire burning upon it. An Augur, in his priestly robes, is standing beside the altar. On the right, a portion of the massive wall surrounding the gardens is visible. Rude steps of hewn stone make it possible to scale the wall, and look out over the city. On the left there is a fountain. In the foreground are statues and flowering plants.

*Silius enters, in the character of Mars, followed by a
few unarmed friends and attendants. His helmet,
sword, and spear are carried behind him by slaves.*

Immediately after his entrance, MESSALINA *rises from
the sea, as Venus Aphrodite. As she steps on shore,
her attendant nymphs fling some light draperies
about her, leaving her person still partially dis-
closed.*

Silius meets MESSALINA, *and leads her before
the Augur, who bows low as they approach.*

Chorus of Nymphs.

Rejoice, rejoice, the age of woe
    Is past; hail, happy reign!
No blood forever more shall flow,
    Save holy victims slain.

With pinions flashing from on high,
    The gods their heralds send;
They come to dry man's weeping eye,
    His wandering steps to mend.

O'er all the world they swiftly dart,
    And every throb of pain,
Each thought of sadness, every smart,
    Each pleasure's sullen stain,

They gather quickly in a flock,
    And drive them on before,
These evermore from light to lock
    On Pluto's twilight shore.

Hail, happy reign! Hail, blessed pair!
   Late, late may ye return
To where forever, high in air,
   Your mingled light shall burn!

Chorus of Male Attendants.

   Pleasure of beauty,
   Pleasure of strength,
   Now for the first time
   Wedded at length;
   Passion of giving,—
   Burning and living,—
   Passion of taking,
   Longing yet quaking;
   Power of thirsting,
   Love's shackles bursting,
   Power of slaking
   From the waves waking,
   Hail to ye! hail to ye!
   Life has no veil to ye—
   In your embraces
   The lives of all races
   Exhale!
   Hail to ye! hail to ye!
   Nations shall quail to ye!
   Hail!

Both together.

I.

Hark to the whisper far o'er the sea!
Murmurs of distance, echoes of glee,
Hearts that have eagerly waited to see
Gladness and peace by this moment set free.

II.

The wild beauty, passion, power,
Of this mystic nuptial hour,
Speeding on from clime to clime,
Through the realms of future time,
Shall make many a pulse to thrill,
Many a human eye to fill,
Even as long as man shall be
Subject to Love's mastery.

III.

Hail to ye! hail to ye!
Joy never fail to ye!
Find in the hearts of your people your home,
Hail to ye! hail to ye!
Nations shall quail to ye!
Hail to ye, noble possessors of Rome!

SILIUS, *to the Augur, who has gazed steadfastly up
at the sky, and shuddered.*

What made you start?

AUGUR.

I saw a flock of birds.

SILIUS.

How did they fly, towards the right, or left?

AUGUR.

I cannot tell. I may have been mistaken.
My eyes are not as young as they once were,

Nor are my nerves.—I think I was deceived;
But somehow these wild marsh birds flitting by
Gave me a shock. Let us proceed at once.

SILIUS.

I know you were deceived; not by your age,
But by your love for us, which makes you anxious,
Painfully on the watch, and overstrained,
Fearful of some mischance. We will proceed.
The private contract has been signed, and all
The strict formalities have been complied with.
It now remains to read the sanctioning act
Of Claudius Drusus, and to ask the gods
To bless and guard this union; then we shall
Consult the auspices with sacrifice.
Is all prepared for sacrifice?

AUGUR.

It is.

SILIUS, *to* MESSALINA.

Have you the document, Valeria?

MESSALINA.

Yes.

She hands the parchment to SILIUS, *who gives
it to the Augur.*

AUGUR, *reading.*

*Be it known that I, CLAUDIUS CÆSAR, being High
Priest of Rome, as well as Emperor, do hereby,
from this day forth, renounce and utterly annul
my marriage with the Empress, VALERIA MESSA-
LINA, in order to avert an omen of the gods, which
foretells danger to her husband; and I hereby be-
stow her hand in marriage upon CAIUS SILIUS, the
consul elect, calling upon all men to do her honor,
as great as heretofore, and to acknowledge him as
her only true and lawful husband.*

*Signed by my own hand this third day of the Kalends
of October, in the eight hundred and first year of
the City.*

TIBERIUS CLAUDIUS DRUSUS CÆSAR.

SILIUS.

This shall be cut on plates of brass, and hung
In public places. It is tantamount
To an act of abdication. That is plain.
There is no room for doubt. All men can see
That we have had the empire thrust upon us.
　　　Turning to MESSALINA *and kneeling.*
And therefore I salute you first, Valeria,
Mistress of Rome, and doubly Empress now!

MESSALINA.

I hail you, Cæsar!—husband, lover, friend,
Master of me and of my empire!

ALL.

Hail!

SILIUS.

And now, most noble Augur, we beseech you
To sacrifice to the immortal gods;
And, having looked upon the sacred victim,
To give us happy omens for our union.

The Augur retires behind the altar.

The full Chorus, chanting slowly, a mezza voce.

O sacred gods, look down
From heaven with gentle eyes!
And here with happy omens crown
This heartfelt sacrifice.

Oh, answer tenderly
The prayers we send above,
That all mankind may joy to see
The power of perfect love.

Bless these loved ones of Time
In their completest hour;
Oh, shed your lasting peace sublime
On this new birth of power!

The Augur reappears, greatly agitated.

Great Silius, or Cæsar, I should say,
The omens are not what I had expected.
They have appalled—I mean that the aspects
Are not like any I have ever seen.

It may be that some slave has touched the victim,
Or some impurity, or some mistake
May have produced it. I will try again.

> *A sound is heard on the right, as of distant
> confusion in the city.*

SILIUS.

What is that noise?

MESSALINA.

       'Tis nothing of importance,
Only some revellers. Let us go on,
And then the moment that the Augur gains
The omens we desire, we can go
And dance and feast. I will transform these nymphs
Into Bacchantes, laughing, supple things,
With flowing hair and vines and scanty garments,
And you can deck——

SILIUS.

       I do not like that noise;
There is commotion in it.

       To an attendant.

       Mount the wall,
And tell us what you see and hear from there.

       Attendant scales the wall.

MESSALINA.

Well, what is it?

ATTENDANT, *from the wall.*

I see a dreadful storm
Gathering at Ostia!

A faint rumble of thunder is heard.

There is fighting, too,—
I know there is—but it is hidden—it is
Behind the houses——

The sounds of violence grow louder.

It is coming nearer—
They are killing—— Save yourselves! fly for your
    lives!
The soldiers are upon us!

*The Augur slips away. The attendants scatter
in different directions.*

MESSALINA.

I must go.

SILIUS.

And leave me here to perish?

MESSALINA.

There is still
A single chance for us to save ourselves,
And then begin again to love and live.
One hope alone—I *must* go! I must fly
To Claudius! If I can succeed—If I
Can once get near him—You know what a power
My will has over his. Besides, the sight
Of me will make my influence——

SILIUS.

You are

My wife, and I would rather suffer death
Than see you taken back by Claudius;
Winning his mercy by your amorous wiles,
Making your charms my ransom. But, besides,
The plan is hopeless. Let us make great speed,
And fly at once to the Prætorian camp.
Geta is for us—he is ready now—
There we will offer all that they can wish,
Make a harangue, declare a regency—
The game is ours if we have nerve to win it.

VALENS *staggers in mortally wounded. He sways
about and sinks to the ground.*

SILIUS, *supporting* VALENS' *head.*

Call a physician! The poor boy must not die—
He's faint from loss of blood—he may be saved.

VALENS.

No, let me be—the cut is deep—I'm dying—
They stabbed me near the gate. Geta's displaced—
All's lost.

MESSALINA.

Silius, I know there is one chance;
I feel that I can save you!

She disappears.

VALENS, *trying to stretch out his arm towards her.*

>   Do not go—
I have crawled here—only to see your face
Once—once——

>   *Dies.*

SILIUS.

What, did you dare to love her, too?
>   *Shrinks away from the body.*

Your pallid face of death demands my pardon;
But it is hard to grant it to you.
>   *Enter a centurion.*

CENTURION.

>   Come!

SILIUS.

The slaves have fled, and borne away the weapons
Which I brought here in sport,—but if I had them,
I'd show you desperate earnest.

CENTURION.

>   It would be
But courage wasted. I am one of many—
>   *Soldiers enter.*
You see them here. Once more I tell you, come!

SILIUS.

Whither?

CENTURION.

To your own house. My orders are
To keep you there until the Emperor
Returns from Ostia, and makes known his wishes.

SILIUS.

I meant to use my victory for good,
And so I have some little foothold left—
Something to rest upon. I meant to win
Freedom for Rome and for myself—and now—
Now that my youth and life are leaving me—
I still can bear it as it is; for death
Is but a sterner name for liberty.

Exit, guarded.

SCENE III.

The Ostian way, near Rome.

*The city is visible in the distance. In the foreground,
on the right, is a small inn. CLAUDIUS appears in
his carriage; NARCISSUS is seated beside him; CAL-
LISTUS is driving, and HALOTUS is in front with
CALLISTUS.*

CLAUDIUS.

Let us stop here a moment; from this hill
We can see Rome. Tell me, can you descry
Any rebellious troops, or any horsemen
Coming this way? If you see any—why—
I think I shall give orders to turn round,
And drive full speed towards Ostia.

NARCISSUS.

       Cæsar, listen,
I beg of you, implore you, only hear
What I am saying! for your powerful mind
Can grasp the whole affair if you will hear me.
I say the worst is over, you are saved.

CLAUDIUS.

Narcissus, tell me truly, am I still
The Emperor! Does Silius still remain
A private citizen?

NARCISSUS.

      Take courage, Cæsar!
You only have to show yourself in Rome
To splendidly complete the victory
Which we have well begun; for Silius
Is now a prisoner, and the cause of all,
The Empress—the late Empress, I should say—
Has fled from your just anger. No one knows
Where she is hiding, but it makes no matter,
You are again supreme. Let us push on
To Rome.

CALLISTUS.

   Cæsar, that was your master-stroke,
That move of taking the command away
From Geta, and bestowing it upon
Narcissus.

NARCISSUS.

Yes, that is the only thing
That saved us. Through my proxy I was able
To capture some, and kill some more; but now
I ought to be in Rome to take command.
Drive on, Callistus.

CLAUDIUS.

Stop a moment, first!
Halotus, go and bring me from the inn
Some wine. Oh, good or bad—unwatered, and
The strongest there. I feel a little faint.
I'm very tired.

CALLISTUS, *to* NARCISSUS.

Your last messenger
Gave us no news of Messalina, though
I questioned him most carefully. I wish
We knew about her. She may be at sea,—
Though that seems hardly probable,—or else,
She may be in the country with her slaves.
Have you the least idea where she lies hidden?

NARCISSUS.

Deep in the purlieus, I suppose. She has
Some queer friends who know sequestered places.
We shall not see her till we drag her out.

CLAUDIUS, *who has taken the wine.*

The wine has done me good. Now I am ready.
                    Enter MESSALINA.

CALLISTUS.

We are all lost!

NARCISSUS.

Dash on, drive over her!

CLAUDIUS.

Stop! I am Cæsar! Harm her, and you die!
She is my wife, and I will hear her speak,
Though it should cost me Rome!

MESSALINA.

　　　　　　Cæsar, I come,
Not as a frightened, guilty suppliant,
With wild heroics and vain cries for mercy,
But simply as your wife, your true wife still—
Erring and faulty (you of your great goodness
Can pardon that)—but here I swear to you
I never meant you harm, and in this matter
I am not guilty of a single deed
Which you could call a crime. The marriage act
You signed yourself. 'Twas simply to avert
An evil omen; and when all the rites
Had been performed, I thought that Silius,
Who was and is your friend—Give me some wine!
I'm dizzy!　　　　　　　　*They hesitate.*

CLAUDIUS.

　　　You must see that she is faint—
Give her the wine!　　　　　　*She drinks.*

MESSALINA.

I thought that Silius
Might be made useful to you, by my giving
To him just power enough to take from you,
Only the baser part, the petty care,
The thankless burden of the empire.

CLAUDIUS.

Yes,
It is a burden.

MESSALINA.

I intended solely
To make him the enforcer of your will,
That you might rule through him, and he might be
A constant comfort to you and a shield
To guard you from the shocks, the anxieties,
The ceaseless dread you dwell in from the plots
Of just such slaves as these.

NARCISSUS.

Immortal Cæsar!
I beg, beseech you, by the immortal gods,
Your friends and fellows, place no trust in her!
She is a living menace to you; for
She meant to overthrow you utterly,
And make her paramour the Emperor.
She still has many partisans. Who knows?
Some may be hiding near us. Hear me, Cæsar,
Or we are lost! Oh, hasten on to Rome,
And leave her here to meet her punishment!

MESSALINA.

Do not believe this man—he is the creature
Of a court faction which, if it succeeds,
Will compass your destruction, and will shock
The whole world by its deeds of violence.
He is as true a seed of blood and ruin
As ever grew in Rome.

CLAUDIUS, *pointing to* NARCISSUS.

                    I cannot think
That one I know so well can be as bad
As you would have me think; but then, again,
The same most probably applies to you:
You may not be, perhaps, so innocent
As you would prove yourself; but still I feel
That I have judged you harshly.

MESSALINA.

                         Oh, indeed
You have! But my whole heart is overflowing
With love and gratitude, now that I see
That you can pity me.

NARCISSUS.

To MESSALINA, *getting between her and the
Emperor, and speaking rapidly.*

                    Hush! Listen,—quick!
If you will trample all your scorn in the dust,
Recant, renounce the past, divide from Silius,—
If you will love me, in a single word,—
I think I still can save you.

MESSALINA.

             Never! For
The more I fall, the more I see how deep
You lie below me—scarcely visible—
A spot, a stain!

CLAUDIUS.

        What is the Empress saying?
NARCISSUS, *springing to* CLAUDIUS'S *side.*
She offers me her love, if I will stab you!

CLAUDIUS.

Drive on to Rome, or we are lost! You wretch!
And when I tried so hard to save you, too!
May the gods bring about your speedy ruin!
     They drive away, followed by a few straggling
      attendants.

MESSALINA.

Oh, I am doomed! Stop, Cæsar, stop, turn back!
It is a lie! What, are they gone,—all gone—
Not one remaining? No, it cannot be!

                 Looks around wildly.

Yes, yes, it is—there is a viewless gulf
Between me and mankind. Will no one cross?
Not one, of all who said they worshipped me!
The rapid tide of empire and of love,
Wealth, honor, happiness, hope, passion, life,
Has ebbed away, and left me stranded here.
Oh, would to heaven, Silius, that I

Had yielded to your wisdom! It is now
Too late. Too late! Oh, what a dreadful word!

More wildly.

Does my mind wander? What is this I feel?
Alone—and yet I am no more alone!
The powers of Hades gather round my soul—
I feel their influence. Can this be death,
Or is it prophecy? I gaze far down
Into the inmost depths of Hell. From there
The lurid flames of Phlegethon shoot up,
And boil around my spirit. In the glare
I see the future. Cæsar, 'tis your turn—
Do not you taste the poison in your cup?
And you, Narcissus, does your heart enjoy
The pressure of your dagger's point,—I see
They meet? And Agrippina, too! In vain
You struggle, madam, you are choking. Oh!
No, not Britannicus,—no, not my child!

Reels dizzily and falls.

ACT V.

SCENE I.

SILIUS's *house.*

SILIUS, *alone, in a dejected attitude.*

This neutral time, which is not life or death,
Is even worse than death. It is a dull,
Persistent, growing anguish. It is as if
Some corpse cast up upon the shore and left
To rot there, could behold the world around,
And hear the children's voices singing near,
And women crooning while they mend the nets,
And feel the winds and waves, and watch the gulls,
And feel the heels of the rough fishermen
Trample its bones. My mind and nerves and strength
Tremble beneath this strain—this horrid sense
Of being in a world that is not mine—
Living yet dead. If anything could try
The courage, it is this! If I could act!
If I could only get a sword, and die
Cutting them down before me! I might fly—
This house is not especially well guarded—
I think it might be possible. But whither?
There is no place to fly to—all the world
Belongs to Rome, and Rome belongs to those
Who pull the puppet Claudius—that confused

Assemblage of outworn and damaged thoughts,
That living yesterday. Even years ago
No one could fly—look at the fate of Pompey—
The moment that he landed, though it was
Far off in Africa, he met his death.

> *Enter* CLAUDIUS, *disguised as a centurion and*
> *followed by a number of soldiers.*

I know your business. I am ready.

CLAUDIUS.

                              No,
You cannot know it, for we hardly know it
Ourselves. That is, I mean, the Emperor
Has sent us here to say—what was it that
He sent us here to say? Oh, yes, I have it.
He says your life is justly forfeited
Through your attempt against himself, he being
Your ruler, and besides your friend. It was
An ugly business, Silius. I will wager
That Cæsar would have given you anything,
Honor and power and gold; and shut his eyes
Even to your failings, if you had been open
And fair with him, and asked him honestly
For what you wished, and had not cruelly
Plotted against him in the dark, and tried
To ruin an old friend, and take away
His empire and his life.

SILIUS.

                    I never tried
To take away his life, and never meant to.

CLAUDIUS.

What, then you had some feeling for him still?
You had not quite forgotten the old kindness.
I'm glad to know that much; but tell me, Silius,
What are your feelings now towards Claudius Cæsar,
What do you think of him?

SILIUS.

                              'Tis not for you,
In your inferior station, to inquire
What I may think; but yet I mean to tell you.
It cannot make much difference now to me—
My time is short. He is a man who has
More mind than will, by far, and much more will
Than courage; for he makes himself appear
Even weaker, and much duller than he is,
To placate opposition. He is ruled
By those who have no breadth of mind, no learning,
Nothing but will—creatures whom he despises.
If mind were master in this world of ours,
He would be potent; but as character
Is the chief force, he is—well all men know
Just what he is—and yet I always liked him.
He has a certain charm. But I forget,
My voice is out of place among the living,
It sounds unmeaning.

CLAUDIUS.

                    You have given me
A better character than I had hoped for,
Considering how we stand towards each other.
                              He removes his helmet.

SILIUS.

Cæsar!

CLAUDIUS.

Yes, I have come to ask of you
What you desire or hope for.

SILIUS.

Instant death—
I ask you nothing more—I've played my game,
And lost, and I will pay.

CLAUDIUS.

I must admit
That you deserve to die; but so do many
Who are less interesting, and yet live on.
But tell me, what did you intend to do?

SILIUS.

To administer the State with some attempt
At justice mixed with freedom.

CLAUDIUS.

Why, that is
The very thing I have been trying to do,
And found it an ungrateful task. I tell you,
You would have found the weight unbearable.
But that is not the point I wish to know,—
Tell me the whole truth—what did you intend
To do with me? For they do say, you know,
You meant to murder me.

SILIUS.

It is a lie!
You know me well—I shall make no defence
Except to say it is a falsehood.

CLAUDIUS.

Well,
I had some doubts, and so I came myself—
Well guarded, as you see. They all opposed me;
But then Narcissus was away, and so
I managed it. But tell me one thing fully,
What did you mean for me?

SILIUS.

Cæsar, you are
An author above all things, and a man
Possessing the rare gift of knowing books
As friends and comrades, not mere bits of paper.
I meant to give you time, and boundless means
And opportunity to carry forward
Your great works to completion, and to leave
A lasting name behind you.

CLAUDIUS.

Why, that is
Precisely what I should have wished myself.
I find you as intelligent as ever.
How have we revelled in old wine together,
And youthful maidens, and the Grecian classics,—
The only things at once both old and young!
I feel that I have done some wrong to you,
And to—to *her*.

Enter NARCISSUS *followed by* PALLAS; *the
former with difficulty controlling his agitation.*

Narcissus, here,   *taking him aside.*
                        I find
Silius has been maligned in this sad business
He is the same good fellow as before.
I cannot help believing it would be
A good idea to ask him round to supper.
What do you think?

NARCISSUS.

                    I think that if you do,
The scene within an hour will be like this:
Your royal room in horrid disarray,
The arras torn, the table-service scattered,
Lamps overturned, dishes and vases broken,
And you yourself beneath this mass, quite dead,
Your own blood and your own wine running mingled.
It is a horrid thought. I tell you, Cæsar,
That man is gazing on you now as prey,
Prey for the knife. Your life hangs by a hair!
It is not worth a single moment's purchase
While he still lives. Save yourself! Order him
To instant execution.

CLAUDIUS *lets his head fall upon his breast, and
gazes upon the ground, lost in doubtful revery.*

                    Cæsar nods!
That nod which is like Jupiter's, and carries
All things before it. Hale that man away!

Cæsar commands that he be taken hence.

In a lower voice.

Put him to death at once. I will go with you.

Exit Narcissus, *with* Silius *guarded.*

Claudius, *rousing himself from his revery.*

Yes, those were pleasant times. I do not think
That I have ever known more happy hours
Than those we spent in chat and revelry.
But they are gone, and like most things once past
They are unwilling to come back again.
Pallas, I must have wine. I feel depressed.
Can you prepare to-day, at this short notice,
A banquet delicate in its details
And monstrous in proportions?

Pallas.

Cæsar, yes,
I know I can.

Claudius.

Well, you must hurry, then—
Remember this, we will begin quite early,—
Long before dark,—and keep it up until
The cocks shall add their voices to our music.

Exeunt.

SCENE II.

A vast banquet hall in the Imperial palace. In the foreground are massive hewn columns. In the background are golden and silken arras, together with exotic plants, and grape-vines hanging in festoons. Half-way back a table is spread, displaying magnificent preparations for a banquet. Slaves are in waiting.

CLAUDIUS *enters in the guise of Bacchus, followed by bacchantes scantily attired.* NARCISSUS, PALLAS, CALLISTUS, *and* HALOTUS *come in with the Emperor.*

Chorus of Bacchantes.

Eyes, feet, and hearts dance lightly,
  Sorrow forever is fled,
Blown from our view; while brightly
  Sunshine around us is shed.

Grief like a cloud has vanished,
  Leaving no shade on the sward;
Thoughts save of pleasure are banished,—
  The wine-cup displaces the sword.

Coldness is fled, like a vapor;
  Bacchus, with glances of fire,
Kindles love's slight timid taper;
  It flares up, the torch of desire.

Bacchantes and male attendants together.

Hail to thee, our noble master!
  Prince of joy, and god of wine,
Hearts beat lighter, fuller, faster,
  'Neath thy influence divine.

CLAUDIUS, *who is flushed with wine, yet scarcely intoxicated.*

Somehow it seems to me they're out of tune,
Or it may be my nerves. Away with that!
Bring me some wine, I need an ocean of it.
This preparation made to celebrate
My victory is fairly good; but then
We must have seas of wine, and food in mountains:
It takes a sea of wine to quite drown thought,
A mountain, too, of food to smother it.
Halotus, are you ready for the battle?
Have you an appetite? Have you a maw
To-night like Milo's? You will need it. I
Shall keep you tasting at a furious rate,
Dishes on dishes, following endlessly,
Like a succession of Egyptian kings.
Shall you not fail me?

HALOTUS.

Try me, Prince.

CLAUDIUS.

I will.
Glancing around.

It seems to me that something is not right,
That some one is not here who ought to be.
I know now, it is Silius. This has been
An oversight. But we must have him here—
Narcissus, send at once, and ask him.

Narcissus.

                                        Cæsar,
You know, if you will only think a moment
(You who know all things), that by your own orders
Silius has suffered death already. Yes,
And if he were alive now, neither you,
Nor any of us would be here to-day
To hold this feast in honor of your triumph.
His death has saved your throne, and even your life.

Claudius, *abstractedly*.

I had forgotten. But I now remember
The whole from first to last; it all comes back.
I ordered no such thing, but he is dead.
Perhaps it is as well, and yet I cannot
Quite feel that he deserved to die. I miss him
More than I could have thought. He was a man
Different from all these people. And, besides,
His speech was so direct and so incisive—
We had so many things to talk about.
But he is gone; perhaps it is as well.
He was grown very dangerous. I know
His strong will would have preyed upon my spirits.

Turning to Narcissus.

I miss the Empress, too, beyond all thought,—
But that you know. I have heard a report
That in her frenzy,—chiefly caused by fear
For Silius,—she has ended her own life:
Say, is this true?

NARCISSUS.

Cæsar, it is quite true.

CLAUDIUS.

Since it was her own act, there is no help.
It is now manifest she met her fate
Through a fixed purpose of the immortal gods;
But if she were alive, and trembling there
With hope and fear, I would cut Rome in twain
To come to her, and bring her news of safety!
I loved her after all—in spite of all—
It is too late. Come, let us go to supper,—
I must have wine!
> *Moves to the table at the lower end of the hall.*

CALLISTUS, *to* NARCISSUS.

That was a splendid stroke
Of policy!

NARCISSUS.

If he had grown too dangerous,
We, as a last resource, could have informed him
That she is still alive. But now, since he
Believes her dead, and has accepted it,
We near our final triumph. But we must
Be quick,—we have not now a single instant
To waste. Despatch a veteran tribune. You
Know where she is,—the gardens of Lucullus,—
Send him with strict commands to find her there,
And end her life at once. Make haste, be speedy.
> *Exit* CALLISTUS.

My storm-tossed bark, surviving desperate perils,
Is near the haven of established power!
And yet I feel a doubt of what's to come,—
Away with doubt! Revenge and victory!
Valeria, now at last you yield to me,
Bent by my will! Where are your lovers now?
Death is no rival,—you are his and mine!
At length I hold you fast—it is a wild,
Brutal possession, yet possession still!

CLAUDIUS, rising.

What is Narcissus muttering to himself?
Tell him to kneel at once. Kneel, all of you!
If any one is slow, he shall be stabbed,
To hasten him, and bring him down in time.

Valeria Messalina, my dead wife,
Empress, companion, friend, exalted now
To dwell with gods forever, oh, forgive
All my shortcomings, even as I have pardoned
The wrongs I may have had. My sight is cleared.
I now can see not only what thou wert,
But what thou mightst have been. We all of us
Live far below our capabilities.
I love, adore thy memory. Look down
From thy high home, and see, behold, I pour
This rich libation to thy noble soul,—
For it was noble,—flecked and spotted here
By this all-staining world, but born to be
Pure and untarnished. Look on me, I say,
Shed comfort down on my lost, widowed heart,
And on the river-bank of the grim world
Be thou the first to meet me when I come.

SCENE III.

A secluded spot in the gardens of LUCULLUS.

In the foreground there is a bench of stone, and near it a statue of Nemesis. The background is occupied by a clump of ancient cypresses. MESSALINA *is alone.*

MESSALINA.

Oh, will she never come! She has had double
The time it takes to ask some simple questions.
She has had time to make inquiries
And bring me some encouragement, and then
Go back and bring fresh news. It seems to me
I have been here for hours and hours alone.
It has been long enough for my whole life
To pass me in procession, single file,
And every deed to stab me with its dart,
As it passed by. And yet within the world
Close, close around, though far beyond my reach,
They laugh and jest, and sigh with happiness;
And my own life, the life of pleasure, still
Goes on the same, while I in some strange way
Am forced apart and held here by a chain
I cannot see and cannot break. I am
So horribly alone! I feel like one
Who lies upon his couch ill unto death,
And gazes hopelessly with tired eyes
About the room, and sees the shaded lamps,
And the attendants flitting to and fro
With muffled steps—all in such cruel health!

And severed from his isolated woe
By an impassable abyss. I know
That I am doomed, I know there is no hope;
And yet I say the words, and hear them only
As I might hear the crackling of the branches,
Or moaning of the winds, or any sound
In nature, which has not the slightest meaning.

Enter LEPIDA, *who sinks down dejectedly upon
      the bench.*

What news? Have you not good news for me?

LEPIDA.

                                        No.

MESSALINA.

What have you learned?

LEPIDA.

                    It breaks my heart to tell you,
Because there's nothing new; what I have heard
Is simply the dull, crushing confirmation
Of all you partly knew, and all we feared.
Silius is taken, Geta dead already,
Narcissus is commander of the guards—
I cannot put the rest in words. Oh, child!
You know the blow is coming!

MESSALINA.

Walking to and fro with feverish haste.
                    Give me hope!
Give me some counsel, some advice, some plan—
I know there is some plan, some remedy,
If we could find it. Only give me hope!

LEPIDA.

I cannot give you what does not exist,
Valeria.

MESSALINA.

But it does exist, I tell you!
How can you sit there so calm, so contained,
While I am struggling in this awful crisis?
But it is easy for you, after all;
For you are living, and I—I am dying—
That makes a world of difference. If we could
Change places, I should be as calm as you.

LEPIDA.

How can you speak so? If I quite gave way,
What would you have to lean on? My dear child,
I beg you by all heaven and earth to try
To gain some self-control! Think of your race;
Resolve that you will prove yourself at last
Worthy of your great ancestors. That thought
Will make you rise superior even to death.

MESSALINA.

Oh, don't say that! Please do not use that word,
It is a horrid omen.

LEPIDA.

Oh, Valeria,
I cannot speak a word of censure now,
But you can see how your past passions have

Consumed your courage. You must feel and know
That it is nothing but your life of pleasure,
Your living for the senses night and day,
Which makes you now unnerved.

Messalina.

It is not that.
If I had only that upon my conscience
I could be calmer; for love, passion, pleasure,
The giving and receiving of delight,
Is only to some weak, distorted visions
A hopeless crime. Mine was a blasting fault,
I own. But oh, it is not that! It is
My real crimes which terrify my spirit:
Revenge, hate, envy, selfishness, ambition
Ready to trample on another's life
To gain one step in power,—and I did that!
My share in hastening on the unjust death
Of Asiaticus—he died near here—
Near to this spot. I cannot bear this strain,
It will unseat my reason!

Lepida.

My dear child,—
You are my own in spite of everything,—
Do not permit your mind to dwell upon
The changeless past, your best atonement now
Is firmness in this hour, and this dark hour
Brings its one comfort with it, which is this:
When I beheld you reckless, arrogant,
Proud even of your wickedness, I cursed you.

The hour that I foresaw has come, and now
I lift the curse forever, and I pray
The blessed gods to grant you love and pardon,
Even as I love and pardon you.

MESSALINA.

                      Dear mother,
You know I love you; you are the one friend
Who has stood by me in this sickening danger.
It cannot be that I must die so young,
Must cease to be a part of the bright world
Of life and light and love and merriment,
The world I know so well. Show me some remedy.

LEPIDA, *handing her a dagger.*

Here is the only remedy I know.

MESSALINA.

Yes, this is best—farewell!—I cannot do it!
I cannot plunge this bitter, painful knife
Into a breast like this of mine! I must
Think for myself. If I could get to Claudius—
I feel—a something tells me that he is
Relenting now—if I could only come
Into his presence—we will try it! Yes,
That is the single chance.

LEPIDA.

                Stop! do not go:
You will be killed before you reach the palace.

MESSALINA.

That is a supposition. I shall go
At once——   *Enter an attendant.*
            Give me good news or none at all.

ATTENDANT.

Then I must give you none.

LEPIDA.

                        Speak, what is it?

ATTENDANT.

Silius is dead.

MESSALINA, *faintly.*

            That makes it easier; but
'Tis hard, so hard!

LEPIDA.

            Have you more news than this?

ATTENDANT.

Yes, they are coming.

MESSALINA, *wildly.*

            Who?

ATTENDANT.

Look there!
Exit attendant.

*Enter a tribune bearing a drawn sword. At
sight of him, MESSALINA turns deadly pale
and sinks back, half fainting, into her
mother's arms.*

LEPIDA.

I know
What is your ghastly mission. Leave us—go!
She is prepared for death, but she will die
By her own hand. Go back to those who sent you.
Tell them that she is dead—it will be true
Before you reach them. Do not you see plainly
That she is almost dying now?

TRIBUNE.

I cannot.
I have received strict orders; but they are
Hard orders. If I looked upon her face,
It would unnerve me. I must act at once.
To MESSALINA.
Can you forgive me? I am in this matter
A simple instrument. I have no choice.

MESSALINA, *in a hollow voice.*

Yes. I forgive you. All is changed for me:
In these few moments, which have seemed like ages,

My life has passed from me, and slipped away,
Still drifting on, forever, ever on,
Till it is but a little distant cloud.
The world has turned me from its door, and now
I face another portal. All is gone—
Pleasures and passions, hopes and fears and pains,
All save one face, one form, one loving heart,
Filling the universe. Mother, farewell!
Do not forget me, for a time.—Oh, Silius!

> *As the tribune raises his sword in act to strike,
> the scene closes.*

VESTIGIA

COLLECTED POEMS

DEDICATION.

THERE are times in the life of the mind when the forces which hitherto have impelled and supported us upon our way seem to waver; a sudden sense of loneliness attacks us, and the need of some strong intellectual corroboration and support becomes a great and overmastering necessity. To this rule the writer has proved no exception.

Once, when my spirit was thus fainting within me, two great Englishmen, "foster babes of fame," and one great and famous Frenchman, passing by on the other side, came over and stood sympathetically beside me. They bound up my wounds, pouring in the oil and wine of comradeship, and set my panting soul upon its feet again. There is no need that I should name them here. One of them is no more, and the other two will remember when they read these lines, and perhaps feel a passing sense of gratification that to the great and generous three this volume is dedicated.

POEMS WRITTEN IN BOYHOOD.*

* If I allow these, my earliest attempts in verse to take upon them the permanency which type confers, it is not from any sense of their merit, but because I think a man is bound to give as full an account of himself as he can, in order that students of the mind may see an even light falling upon him throughout the whole of life's journey, and not merely a flash here and there, where some attitude has been taken which vanity might suggest to be striking or advantageous.

CONTENTS

CONTENTS

202

AUTUMN (a fragment).

When the butterfly takes his last gay flight
Ere the coming on of Winter's night,
And the cricket chirps a sad farewell
To the golden Summer he loved so well;
When the freshening breezes softly sigh
As leaf by leaf drops silently,
'Tis then sad thoughts flit o'er man's mind,
Thoughts sad, yet dim and undefined
As specters on a midnight sea;

For, gazing on eternity
Man sees that the billows of life are lost,
Broken on death's dark, ice-bound coast;
Man feels that his life ere long must close
And his soul sink down to a deep repose;
Like the 'parted Summer whose playful hours,
Wearied with sport and twining flowers,
Nestling on time's protecting breast,
Sink softly down to endless rest.

LIFE (a fragment).

Is life a vapor? Is't a passing dream?
Alas! 'tis both—A vapor it would seem
Unlighted and unblessed by heavenly beam
Of sunlight;—as a horrid stifling pall
It weighs upon the soul, till a kind call
Sets the poor weary prisoner free; for all
Must meet at length with one whose cooling breath
The vapor melts,—nay, shudder not,—'tis Death.

The dream it is of a poor homeless child
Lost in the labyrinth of some vast, wild
And lonely burial place. He was beguiled
To wander ever on, and soon forgot
That he was lost, and e'en remembered not
The voiceless dwellers in that dreary spot.
Hemlock and nightshade 'midst the moldering tombs
He heedless plucked, yet felt their fatal fumes.

THE BOY'S REVOLT.

I.

MAXIMS and rules,
Ye crutches for fools,
Ye platitudes plastic,
False truths so elastic,
　　All hail!

II.

Ye short-cuts to thought,
With quagmires fraught!
Ye patent nut-crackers,
Black reason's attackers,
　　So stale!

III.

Supports of each bore,
Of his noddle the core,—
While he wriggles and squints,
"Toning down," "neutral tints"
　　Are his themes.

IV.

Leaden tips of those darts
Called "fixed rules for the arts,"
Which sub-editors ragged
Shoot toward the heights jagged
    Where Genius gleams.

V.

Ye help manikins prate,
Calling little men great,
While at all things they rush,
Yet no subject can push
    To its clue.

VI.

Who can hit off no case,
Can decipher no face,
Those with empty names caught,
All who ne'er had a thought
    Worship you.

VII.

Sage stuffings for geese,
The rusty brain's grease,
All idiots' free passes,
Redeemer's of asses,
    Adieu!

FAME.

I.

READER, I know you long for a great name,
Listen and thou shalt have a host of samples
To show how small a price is paid for fame.
Select which e'er thou wilt of these examples;
For all have either given immortality,
Or lent to fame a more enduring quality.

II.

Diogenes bought unsurpassed renown
By sitting in a tub, with many a louse
On back and head, filth serving for a gown—
You surely have a wash-tub in the house!
Herodotus by having a child named History—
Name yours the same, perchance it may do this for ye.

III.

Immortal fame was Clitus' reward
For being by a drunkard stabbed to death.
This means I recommend, as far from hard,
So many sots beset one's daily path—
You only have to ask some friends to dinner;
But this plan scarce will do for a beginner.

IV.

To prove how long a spark may keep in ashes
(And fame's the spark we're busy now about),
See how the name of Herostratus flashes,
With millions nobler quite by time put out.
A feat surpassed with ease by any gander
Sufficed to make a hero of Leander.

V.

Lycurgus made some execrable soup,
But in this branch you'll scarcely beat your cook;
Curtius has won a place amongst the group
By jumping down a pit, without a look
Before he leaped—Plunge headlong down your well,
In it may lurk the selfsame magic spell,

VI.

The great Canute gained an undying fame
By getting wet feet on the ocean's shore.
Thou, reader, doubtless oft hast done the same,
And art thou now more famous than before?
The plan I've tried, though it may end in vapor,
Has been by spoiling pens and soiling paper.

VII.

Amongst the moderns, Wellington is noted
Because, when once he stood upon a hill,
A drunken, filthy, old, debauched, and bloated
Prussian dragoon did an appointment fill,
When he, with waiting, having quite given out,
Was ready to begin his homeward rout.

VIII.

Reader, on thee once more my thoughts do fall—
Loose shaken by the jolting of my verse—
Renown, perchance, thou dost not seek at all,
Contented so thy lot shall grow no worse;
For, as for fame, few greatly long to gain it,
Without the means within them to obtain it.

IX.

Envy the man of limited desire,
Who, piped and mugged, his day's work done, is
    sitting
With outstretched legs before the roaring fire,
His wife, not young, beside him calmly knitting;
Who has not always something by his side
To whisper, "I shall live when you have died."

X.

A book is a *memento mori* drear,
To him who forms, a breathing thing of gloom,
A glass wherein the future doth appear,
A hand which points forever to the tomb;
These are the only ghosts men ever see,—
Their own souls thus before their time set free.

XI.

In speaking to the future we become,
Even of necessity, ourselves the past,
Until identity's a name, the sum
Of life uncertainty—we doubt at last
Whether we are the form that onward strides,
Or that which midst mortality abides.

IMITATION OF DON LORENZO'S THEME AND GLOSS, IN DON QUIXOTE.

THEME.

"Adieu, adieu, my native shore
Fades o'er the waters blue!
The night winds sigh, the breakers roar,
And shrieks the wild sea-mew."

GLOSS.

(The author of the theme is supposed to speak.)

I.

My boat is dancing on the wave
Beneath my vessel's lea;
The ripples of the flood tide lave
The prow which points to sea—
Adieu, dear friends, we meet no more,
Adieu, adieu, my native shore!

II.

The bar is past, all eyes are glad,
But my torn heart grows doubly sad
As cheer the reckless crew;
And as the sun-set waves we skim,
The distant shore, fast growing dim,
Fades o'er the waters blue.

III.

And now the twilight thickens round,
The wave has lost its gold;
While voices from the sea resound
With memories of old:
How oft I've heard on Scotland's shore,
The night winds sigh, the breakers roar.

IV.

The wind which failed with failing light,
Now rushes through the moonless night,
And bears us on anew.
The straining vessel creaks and groans,
The billows dash, the cordage moans,
And shrieks the wild sea-mew.

A DREAM.

I DREAMED that I was old. My weary limbs
Tottered beneath me, yet I strove to climb
A rugged steep upon whose lofty top
There shone a marble temple white as snow.
Column on column, pile on pile was reared,
And yet its stern simplicity bestowed
A beauty mixed with awful majesty.
Methought I saw within. Around its walls
Were niches, and in all, save one, there stood
Statues of marble; but the farthest niche
Was void and empty. In the central aisle,
Suspended by a golden cord, there hung
A golden trump whose blast it seemed might shake
The firm-set mountains. As I gazed, I heard
The shadow of a voice, which seemed to say,
"Press onward"; but I answering said, "To me
Life is most valueless, the weight of years
And dull despair have crushed my youthful hopes.
I once did think that noble fane to reach,
Ambition's torch burned brightly, and could chase
The shadows from my steps; but now 'tis spent,
Mists whirl and gather, darkness round about
Envelops me—yet still I struggle on,
Helpless and hopeless, dying and alone."
Scarce had I spoken, when from out the void
Appeared a face upon whose features calm

Thought boundless, infinite, unspeakable
Was imaged. From its lips there came a voice,
Which said, "Write quickly!" I did sudden seize
A parchment scroll, and with a trembling hand
Traced hasty letters, and when now the page
Was finished, from on high there swept a voice
Sweeter than harp strings, yet more powerful
Than falling torrents, which cried out aloud,
"Bring here the trumpet, to the air I'll fling
A name ne'er known till now in earth or heaven;
For one more name is added." As I gazed,
Into the farthest niche, behold, there sprang
A marble statue bearing on its brows
A wreath of laurel—with a frenzied cry,
" 'Tis I, 'tis I!" I shrieked,—and waked from sleep.*

* How sardonically must the angel of our destiny smile when he glances over our shoulder, in the days of youth's first awakening, and reads these our boyhood's rhapsodies as we pen them. With what grim satisfaction must he place side by side the high and sunny path we have laid out for ourselves, and the storm-enveloped quagmire we are to follow.

MISCELLANEOUS POEMS.

MY MOTHER.

Obiit Nov. 14th, 1884.

Oh, ye who have her with you still,
Where e'er 'mongst men ye dwell,
Oh, bend your stubborn earthly will,
That ye may tend her well!

It may seem long in months and years,
When counted as they come;
But gazing back, the mists of tears
Will bring the distance home.

Oh, let no tender impulse wait,
Waved carelessly away!
They'll faint before to-morrow's gate,
Those love-thoughts strong to-day.

Lest, when that stealthy hour has come
To beckon her away,
Ye stand aghast, despairing, dumb,
With so much left to say!

And on through brambles, thistles, weeds,
O'er memory's fields anew,
Ye fevered search for gentle deeds,
And find them still too few.

Lest in the midnight, year by year,
Ye call one gentle shade
To come and bend a shadowy ear
To speeches never made.

Lest aye in vain the heart that grieves
Would rear a phantom Past,
Where flowers supplant the dry oak leaves
Which rustle in the blast.

TO THE CLOUDS.

UNCERTAIN and deceitful clouds, which change,
Letting each willful wind remold your form!
Emblems of fickleness, the skies ye range,
Smile with the calm, and threaten with the storm;
Blush with the sunset, pale with the pale moon—
Mourners at midnight, revelers at noon!
Have ye no thread of thought which change survives,
And gives connection to your varying lives?
Ye have. Through every change, by night or day,
There lurks some hint of your o'erruling gray—
Else how could I so love you? Am not I,
Like you, a child of Nature's changing sky?
There's not an influence the world contains
But seizes on me as its proper prey,
The plaything of its pleasures and its pains;
Yet soon they lose their hold and fade away,
My heart returns to its inherent hue,
Alas, too somber! And I fear, like you,
Which on the eternal blue no foot-prints leave,
So I, when death my fabric shall unweave,
Shall leave no trace upon Thought's sky serene,
To show where an unquiet soul hath been.

EVENING VOICES.

I.

EVENING voices—listen!
Soft and low they call,
Evening wavelets glisten,
Evening shadows fall.

II.

Homeward they are calling
From our care and sin,
From our burdens galling,
From the pain within.

III.

Hark, the tones are clearer!
Loved ones we have known
Drawing ever nearer
  Once again our own!

IV.

Glances with the starlight mingle,
Eyes that lift our hearts on high;
Voices sound along the shingle,
Whispering love's eternity.

V.

Evening voices,—listen!
Louder now they call,
Waves no longer glisten,
Shadows faster fall.

SONG.

THE moon with her viewless hands,
Transparent, light and free,
Was parting a place
For her dreamy face
To gaze on the troubled sea.

There were bells in wave-washed hands,
Which tolled eternally;
There was roar on roar
Far down the shore,
And laughter out to sea.

There were four on the sands to-night,
Two shadows and two forms—
Behind and before
Flew the froth on the shore,
And foam on the land of storms.

Need shadows, or shapes more light?
O which has the firmer home?
Which stabler stuff,
The moth-like fluff,
Or the bird-like flying foam?

O heart-uniting kiss!
O bosoms beating free!
O eyelids wet
With joy! and yet—
The wild bells out to sea!

Through the languor of the kiss
Which wrapped them tenderly,
Came the steady roar
Far down the shore,
And the laughter out to sea!

AUTUMN LEAVES.

THE leaves lie cold
On the cumbered mold,
Their corpses lie bleached all around
Uninterred where they fall,
Till their whiter pall
By Winter is spread on the ground;

But when March, with his cloud
And his voice so loud,
As he shouts in the leafless tree,
Shall lift with his hand
Their pall from the land
The corpses shall vanished be.

A SONG OF YOUTH.

MIDDLE-AGE, stand aside! on thy hopes there's a
    damper,
There is cold in thy eye, there's a doubt in thy pace—
Stand aside from his path, lest the course thou shouldst
    hamper
Of one who will die, or succeed in the race.

He comes like the wind as it sweeps o'er the reeds
Which cover the marshes so wide and so green;
He leans from his chariot and lashes his steeds,—
Streaming backward his hair and his garments are
    seen.

There is heaven in his eye, there's a light on his brow,
There's a curl on his lip, with the scorn of his pride;
As he cheers to his coursers his heart is aglow,
And he sees not the being who clings to his side.

Fair, fair is her face, as the pond lily's pure,
As it floats o'er its grave in the depths of the stream—
Her glance is bewildered, half timid, half sure—
She has fears for his danger and hopes for his scheme.

Swift as the dews of morning that fade in the loving
    light,
Swift as the words of warning we heard on a by-gone
    night,
Swift as the spray
That floats away,

Before him Fame doth fly—
Her face is a vapor cold and gray,
'Tis her back enchants his eye.

Let him on till he win her, and then he will find
She is dust on the billow and chaff on the wind—
Let him on till he win her, and then he will know
How vain the best efforts of mortals below.

Trembling age, halt away with thy cane and thy
    crutch,
There's a film on thy eye, on thy cheek sits decline—
Away! in his pathway a feather is much,
And he needs all his strength, without hindrance of
    thine.

MORNING.

WHEN morning is breaking,
And light winds are shaking
The tops of the alders that hang o'er the stream;

When, sluggishly drifting,
Their anchors uplifting,
Dark clouds the horizon move slowly along;
When red-tipped and glowing,
With young dew o'erflowing,
Each tree has its chorus, each branch has its song;

Then, midst this emotion,
This happy commotion,
I feel my heart still as the voice of a dream.

My yesterday's treasures,
Love's joys and love's pleasures
Ne'er bade me adieu, but crept softly away.
I've gained but a station
Of gray desolation;
To-morrow looks wan through the mists of to-day.

LINES WRITTEN ON THE MONT CENIS PASS.

Oh, would I were a cloud, to float away!
To the wind's footsteps all my motions timing;
A fleecy cloud, to idly, idly stray,
And watch my shadow o'er the mountains climbing.

With hopes of kisses on each snowy peak,
I'd lure the way-worn shade my course to follow
O'er lofty summits and o'er passes bleak,
Through many a tangled brake and stony hollow.

And thus my soul, to counterpoise the time
When after love and fame in vain she panted,
Should wander endlessly from clime to clime,
Besought, in turn, for gifts for aye ungranted.

Oh, would I were a cloud, to float away!
To the wind's footsteps all my motions timing,
A fleecy cloud, to idly, idly stray,
And watch my shadow o'er the mountains climbing.

THE MOON.

A VEIL of tulle the moon did wear,
As with a floating motion,
She slowly climbed her azure stair,
And gazed o'er earth and ocean.

Her veil of tulle, which fold on fold
In crumpled creases bound her,
The wind caught up, with fingers cold,
And wrapped it closer round her.

With languid, lingering, listless tread,
And air of cold abstraction,
Like one whose thoughts are with the dead,
Forever dead to action,

She slowly climbed a rugged pass
Amidst the hills enchanted,
And disappeared behind a mass
Of rocks the winds had planted.

A CHANT TO ALL POETS.

I.

Poets, living or to be,
Fear not when your frame you see
Yielding to the ceaseless shocks
Which impel toward the rocks,
While time's flood upon your ear
Pours a cadence sinister.
Let not death your spirits move,
So ye love, so ye love,
Thoughts below and clouds above!
So ye love that feeble spark
Which alone combats the dark
In man's bosom, and which never
Bursts to flame; but yet forever
Burns, now dim and now aglow,
As the winds of passion blow.

II.

Though ye fade, your love shall be—
Gaining but a wider sweep
From its lost identity—
Part of earth and air and sea,
Of the blue immensity
That o'erhangs each mountain steep,
Of all thoughts more bold and free
That men's spirits living keep,
Lips that smile and eyes that weep,
Down through time's eternity.

TO DIOGENES IN SEARCH OF AN HONEST MAN.*

SEARCH on, search on, search ever on,
O'er mountain and o'er plain!
'Tis ages since thy quest begun,
Yet 'tis for aye in vain.

When the far-scattered, broken wave
Shall greenly rise again,
And roll from out its whited grave
Back to the open main,

Then shall the heart whose trust has been
Strewed wide along life's shore,
The light and frothy remnants glean
To give it form once more.

But gazing on the woods, the sky,
The sea, the crags, the streams,
We find at last reality
That will not mock our dreams.

* Suggested by Sharp's engraving of the painting by Salvator Rosa.

PASQUALE BRIGNOLI.

(Born in Naples, Jan. 1st, 1824. Died in New York,
Oct. 30, 1884.)

B ereft of voice, a culprit angel wept,
R ebuked and silent 'midst the heavenly host,
I n weary waiting; while his voice was kept
G irt round with human clay—to him quite lost—
N ot in the realm his searching pinions swept.
O n earth the voice charmed all. Then cramped and
        crossed,
L anguished in bonds; but as it felt them sever,
I t sang as erst in Heaven—then fled forever.

OTSEGO LAKE.

DEEP, deep she lies amidst the hills enchanted
Which are a spirit's home;
The undying heart to whom the boon is granted
To lead men's thoughts where his were wont to roam.
Blue are her waters—bluer than the skies—
Blue as her sister lake across the ocean;
The only other lake of earth's which lies,
Like her, enveloped in Art's deep emotion.

Girdled by mountains, winds but stoop
And dip a finger as they hasten by,
Blurring in streaks the waters. Shadows troop,
As fast as hopes, o'er the dark hill-sides green;
But not alone with verdure are they crowned—
They bear a greener memory.
And immortelles her rocky banks around,
The pallid flowers of Fame, are thickly seen,
Which, bloodless, pure, yet living, seem to say,
"We spring from that which cannot pass away!"

THE LITTLE FADED FLAG.

How soft the evening tints upon the hills!
Shadings of blue, which to the mountains cling
As hearts to home. The mingled sound of rills
Blesses the silence. Half way down the steep
Stretches the village burial ground, where sleep
The memories which once were men. All ills,—
Sorrow and strife, rage, envy,—shrink away,
Deprived of sustenance, before the gray
Of these low walls. Oft passing children bring
Fresh flowers for the graves, with loving wills;
And sculptured stones have many a charge to keep.
But one there is neglected and apart—
Left he no vacancy in any heart?
No epitaph, no name, no date, no care!
The mound a heap of stones, which had been bare,
Save for some grass in matted masses green,
And golden-rod, and asters sparsely spread
In pity of its nakedness. Below,
O'ergrown with weeds, a mimic flag is seen,
Stuck in the mold.—Though bleached by many rains
And many Summer suns, it still retains
A faded hue of blood—the blood he shed—
His own and others', dashed o'er many plains—
The blood which still emits a living glow.
Forget who will, his flag forgets him never!
True to the true her motto is forever—
Still smiles immortal o'er his weed-grown grave
The little faded flag he died to save.

IN MEMORY OF THE SISTER (Real) CAT.

Obiit Feb. 1st, 1897.

I.

THE "Real" cat was strong and sleek,
Of active paw and mind;
The "Sister" cat, by nature meek,
Was of a gentler kind.

II.

Her black a rusty brown became,
Her tail was sadly bent;
But then her mind was bent the same,
Toward a high intent.

III.

She vowed to toil by night and day
With one sole aim in view—
To win her master's heart to say,
"This cat is real, too."

IV.

Upon his justice was her stake,
She felt it would not fail her,
If only she could humbly make
Her humble gifts avail her.

V.

And so each morn she brought her mouse,
And laid it at his door,
And mewed and said, "Open the house,
Come, see, I have one more!"

VI.

And oft when hastening on his way,
The stables passing by,
Her master heard her mew, and say,
With plaintive, following cry,

VII.

"Wait, wait, you leave me far behind,
My legs are short, please wait;
Go slower, for I have in mind
To catch you at the gate.

VIII.

"I'll help you plant the beets, or go,
And perched upon a wall,
Will watch the cattle just below,
And help you count them all."

IX.

At last one day her master said
"This cat is real, too,
Her crown is won, all doubt is fled
Her heart is great and true."

X.

And then that grizzly angel form,
Whose touch turns thought to clay,
Espied her on a night of storm,
And beckoned her away.

XI.

Her master's heart, in turn, was true—
She keeps her place apart,—
That little shape whose short life grew
A teacher of the heart.

XII.

And now, that he remains alone,
That he is "left behind,"
He knows he never spoke one tone
That she could deem unkind.

BARCAROLLE.

(Music by A. S. L.)

I.

Far glides our bark o'er the moonlighted surges,
Spite of the dimness 'tis hope that her urges;
Deep as she dips, she as often emerges,
Light as the froth of the restless sea.

II.

Restless our hearts, though we look to the morrow,
Sighs from the past present laughter will borrow;
From the far shore comes an accent of sorrow,
Borne o'er the wake in our dusky lee.

III.

CHORUS.

We are rowing, aye rowing,
With melody sowing
The winds, while the billows in concert are flowing.
We are rowing, aye rowing,
With oar-tips all glowing;
But still from the shore sweeps the strain—
      Sad refrain!

IV.

SOLO.

Hopes flit before me forever.
Vague the reward of endeavor.
Slowly from all things I sever,
Save memory's wraith alone.

V.

Suns ne'er shall rise on this gloaming
Through which my spirit is roaming—
Still gleams where Time's waves are foaming
The path where thy soul hath gone!

A LETTER TO MY AUNT, MISS ANN WISTER OF VERNON.

I.

My dear Aunt Annie, I must write to you
To tell you what we are and are not doing.
The former's easy, for since Time first flew
From out his nest, there ne'er was place so gluing
To all the energies and efforts, too,
Of body and of mind.—This last I'm showing
By writing you a soporific letter,
Which you must read at night to sleep the better.

II.

The life we lead is in the main aquatic—
Row, sail and fish, from morn till dewy eve.
These dews are things which make us all rheumatic—
'Tis a sad fact o'er which I duly grieve.
But then they soothe the nerves; for no lunatic
In this dull heavy air could wildly live—
Just one more proof of life's fixed compensation,
Where everything is dealt as a "mixed ration."

III.

But I'm digressing—'tis a great relief!
Why cannot one digress a bit from living?
'Twere surely a great boon, when worn with grief,
And weary with the never-ceasing diving
In others' minds for thoughts which, to be brief,
They never had,—and with the constant giving
Of love in vain,—to close life's book, indeed,
Yet mark the place, should we wish more to read.

IV.

But to return: Our life, too, is bucolic—
When the wind's East you may cut off the bu—
Then you will need a mixture alcoholic—
(I have a tipple here would please even you,—
Who are particular). It is no frolic
To feel as I have for a day or two;
But now the wind is West, and I feel stronger,
And shall stay dawdling here for some time longer.

V.

I want to stay and see them cut the clover.
Its dark green stretches far as you can see;
Its bloom is ripening fast, and dots it over
With a bright pink, the Mecca of the bee.
The partridge loves its edges, near the cover—
His "Bob White" now is faintly borne to me—
'Twill be a pretty sight, those fifty acres,
When covered with the hay-cocks and hay makers.

VI.

Perhaps, 'tis fairer now. I love its green—
There are so many greens here! Far away
The marshes spread their light and living sheen;
The maples stretch, more somber, toward the Bay
(Whose line of blue from here is plainly seen);
Beyond the marsh, against the horizon gray,
The dark and solemn cedars massed are found
To give the landscape's thought a tinge profound.

VII.

But I shall bore you with my farmer's talk.
It would be more amusing, I admit,
If here there were some maid with whom to walk,
Or row, or on the Hammock* beach to sit,
And whisper low and sigh, and on life's stalk,
Which is but barren, fasten, bit by bit,
Bright flowers—artificial, but well made—
In fact the only kind which do not fade.

VIII.

Good-by, good-by, I have no more to say,
Save that I'm out of joint and cannot find
The person to reset me. Every day
The being used to rise before my mind

---

* Kitt's Hammock, once called Kidd's Hummocks, from a prevailing
notion that Captain William Kidd, the famous pirate, had buried treasure
there. The belief still exists, having outlived the name.

Ever deceived; but now I'm getting gray—
The day is o'er whose brightness made me blind—
None such I hope to meet—I've dropped the strife
    of it—
Well, if I did, I'd lead them a dog's life of it.

IX.

At last good-by in earnest. Think of me
As one who thinks of you, or far or near;
You are the link which binds me tenderly
To a sweet past which grows but doubly dear
As it recedes; in you I fondly see
A heart whose course my own would fondly steer.
Give love, a peck or two, to sweet Miss Fanny,
And keep a bushel, my good, kind Aunt Annie.

HEARTBEATS.

(A humble imitation of the hysterico-æsthetic in
verse.)

I.

O DROOPING stalks of asphodel!
Thrummed by the wanton wind,
Is he then so unkind
That ye thus mourn?
Or is your sorrow born,
Like mine, of some soft wind-enchanted spell,
Some moon-flecked, night-born power
Which holds my spirit in this very hour!

II.

No more I roam by cool drop-trickling grot,
Nor slippery slope, nor sun-kissed meadow wide—
They may be there, and yet I find them not,
The sweet-throated feathered denizens of wood and
    mountain side.

III.

I tread the mazes of the dense and prickly cover,
And find no plover
To cheer me with his pipe.
I see no snipe
Flit lightly by me through the forest shades;
And when I leave the glades,
And dreamy wander o'er the broad, smooth fell,—
Starred with the poppy and sweet asphodel,—
No woodcock springs aloft to break the spell
Of my imprisoning fancies.—Oh, I may not tell
If now I am, or was a lover!

IV.

A soft cool hand,
Deep incandescent eyes,
Which are not of the land,
Nor ocean, nor sweet ever-jeweled skies—
Yet have their phantoms in each toying breeze,
In every dewy leaf—
These nurse my tender grief,
These cast a sightless band
Around my captive musings, these—
Lo, I see them there!
And yet my outstretched arms
Encircle not thy charms,
But only hold the incense-laden air.

LINES TO THE CLASS OF 1870, OF YALE, UPON THE TWENTIETH ANNIVERSARY OF ITS GRADUATION.*

INVOCATION.

Spirit of Truth (my greatest merit),
Spirit of Justice (few revere it)!
Spirit of Proof (yclept proof-spirit)
Bless ye the theme I am inditing,
And guide my hand while I am writing!

Aid me ye Muses, sacred nine,
Pickle my page in Attic brine,—
Who can amuse without a Muse?
And I with "egotistic news"
And bits of truthful history,
And amorous episodes, must try
To make your moments carol by,
And make you glad you are not I.
Alas, who treads a doubtful path
Some fury licks him with her lath,
And all who seek to love or shine
Find sorrows with their joys entwine.—

Echo.—Wine!

* This poem was written in answer to a class circular containing a request, apropos of the anniversary, for material for a class history, and containing, too, the regulation amount of enforced bonhommie and ponderous jocularity.

ARIA.

Allegro Appassionato.

I.

On leaving our college,
As stuffed full of knowledge
As even our "Birdie"* can stuff out a bird,
I hastened home gladly;
My father was mad, he
Made many remarks I reluctantly heard.

II.

But I had my learning,
Gained where it is burning,
And shedding forever its radiance afar—
I knew how to gamble,
I knew how to "sample,"
I knew a neat ankle, I knew a cigar.

III.

I'd bet and I'd reveled;
The edges were beveled
From off every corner my innocence had.
As sworn priest of beauty,
I had made it a duty
To kneel at all shrines, whether jocund or sad.

* George Bird Grinnell, the well-known writer and ornithologist.

IV.

At the high noon of night
I had basked in the light
Of dark eyes made to flicker and flash by my prayers;
Our lips closely meeting,
Our hearts closely beating,
While a bucket, our guardian, stood on the dark
    stairs.

V.

And yet, upon leaving,
I should be deceiving
To tell you my mind could conceive nothing more;
I felt a desire
To stir up the fire
Which smouldered and smoked in my heart's inmost
    core.

VI.

Whatever I've done, sirs,
Has not been for fun, sirs,
But breathless and dizzy upon a dark road,
I've trudged on in pain, boys,—
I fear, too, in vain, boys,—
Urged on by a spirit with fiery goad.

RECITATIVE.

"What have I done," kind friends, since leaving you?
I've worked and dreamed, and thought a little, too.
I've traveled much; have gazed o'er Rome's Cam-
     pagna,
And strolled through galleries where hang full many a
Such pigment form as master hands depict—
I like them, for they never contradict.
I've watched the tendency in modern art
To cater to the head, and starve the heart,
Until the voices in the "music-drama"
Reflect the man who howls the panorama.
I've seen Gambetta's structure for the free
Sink to a petty Jewish tyranny.
At home, I've seen a Congress aid each steal,
Both great and small, yet flout the public weal;
And gulp wild, wanton, infamous expense,
Yet strangle over national defence;
And stab and punish with the Pension's knife
The State for having battled for its life.
I've seen a new morality arise,
Spreading, as cirrus clouds invade the skies,
Which teaches that to steal is wholly venial,
And honesty the virtue of a menial.
I've seen a tendency in government
To gain a scope for which 'twas never meant,
And meddle everywhere, direct, administer,
With heavy hand, and mind confused and sinister—
So socialism seems "to have the call,"
That happy state where each is owned by all.
But I forget, the circular demands
Pure egotism; I yield to its commands.

I am a farmer, plethoric and staid,
Because that *pays* the best of any trade.
I have some ruddy children of the brain,
Whose advent cost me no slight throes of pain.
I have a son, besides, who plays sound cricket,
Can "hit to leg," and "cut" and guard his wicket;
And bowls a shooting ball so swift and true,
It takes your wicket, or it cripples you.
I have some acres and, besides, some aches;
A guardian angel, too, whose light forsakes
His eyes, and who with lips and breath grown cold,
Breathes in my ear that I am getting old.

FINALE.

Andante.

Farewell! To me your life is ever young,
I see you only as in days of yore.
From me are hid the sorrows which have clung
About your steps and entered at your door—
And you *are* young! your life is half before;
May you pass through the vista gloriously!
May you, in thoughts, live double your four score;
May all your joys come flashing wild and free,
And sorrows faint as starbeams filtered through the
   sea.

LINES ON THE CAMPAIGN OF 1888.

THE fight is o'er, the battle lost and won,
Dark clouds are lowering, and the night is near;
The army of the victors has begun
To send up cheer on cheer.

With clash of steel, in serried ranks they stand,
And proudly gaze about on every side,
O'er all the coveted and conquered land
Which they shall soon divide.

Across the vale, the beaten host retreating
Moves heavily along in disarray;
No fifes or trumpets sound, no drums are beating—
How still they steal away!

But on their broken lines and banners tattered,
As up the steep all wearily they plod,
From out a cloud, athwart their legions scattered,
There falls the smile of God.

The smile of God, prophetic of the hour
When the dark night of rapine dread shall cease,
And truth and right and justice shall have power
To lead the way to peace.

HORACE'S ODE TO POSTUMUS.
Lib. II, Ode XIV.

I.

Swift fall the years on us, Postumus, Postumus,
Wrinkles and age both refuse to delay;
Piety prays, but her labors are lost to us,
Fetterless death to retard for a day.

II.

Not if a bull every day in the year
You should offer to Pluto, the pitiless king,
Who Geryon, Tityon, holds with a drear
And three-folded river, a watery ring.

III.

We are Earth's, and whatever our gift or our mark
    on it,
Still to this river necessity brings;
This stream we must meet, must approach, must em-
    bark on it,
Dust-sprinkled rustics, or gold-spangled kings.

IV.

In vain our avoidance of merciless war,
And the wide washing sweep of hoarse Adria's flow;
In vain in the Autumn we hasten afar
From the winds which bring sickness and death when
    they blow.

V.

We must view, yes, we must, if we will it or no,
The daughters of Danaus; and coil upon coil
Cocytus so black in its lingering flow;
And Sisyphus cursed to his limitless toil.

VI.

An eternal adieu to thy house, to thy lands,
To thy spouse so adored; and of trees which thou hast
Made to flourish and grow by the work of thy hands,
The grim cypress alone shall be near thee at last.

VII.

A worthier heir thy Caecuban wine
Shall waste, though 'tis kept 'neath a hundred keys;
And vintages fit for the priests when they dine
Shall stain thy mosaics, like valueless lees.

TO THE MOON.

Dweller of the middle distance
'Twixt Eternity and Time,
Craving of our Earth assistance,
Though thy steps the heavens climb,

Hovering round us like the sea-bird,
While the clouds, in eddying foam,
Still beneath thee drift to leeward,
Dashing, breaking, as they roam—

Thine is not the icy gleaming
Of the pallid stars sublime,
Cold thou art, but yet thy dreaming
Feels the presence near of Time.

Near enough to see our troubles,
Far enough to have no share
In the ever breaking bubbles
Of the ocean of despair—

Earth's beneath and Heaven above thee,
Yet for neither dost thou yearn;
All of earth to make us love thee,
Naught to love us in return.

A NEW YEAR'S ODE.

I.

BLOW out wild whistles to the sky,
Make the stars tremble with afright,
The year is dying fast to-night,
Blow, madly blow, blow him sky high!

II.

Blow till ye drown those pealing bells,
They speak but of the out-worn Past,
A world which could not sell so fast
As we.—Away with useless spells!

III.

Blow out the candle of Romance,
No blast the electric light need fear;
The life mechanical is here,
All else needs but a passing glance.

IV.

Blow thought and feeling to the winds,
Time-wasting flutterings of the heart,
Business must guide the hand of Art,
Profit gives foot-hold firm for minds.

V.

Blow in the false, blow out the true,
It will not catch the passing eye,
Blow in the "slick," blow in the sly,
Blow in the Gospel of the New.

VI.

Blow in the Gospel new of Gain,
Blow out the soul's annoying light;
Blow in the great commercial night,
Vast twilight of the oppressor's reign.

TO "NO MAN'S FRIEND."

(A reach of Jones' Creek, Delaware.)

I.

WHO loves thee not, would call thee, "No Man's
    Friend,"
That contumacious and reëntrant bend
Where those who inland sail, with a fair breeze,
Swing head to wind, and lose way by degrees,
And then must "track" or tow, with shoulders sore;
And where those scudding toward the sea, before
A West wind, suddenly are ta'en aback—
All hands must go ashore, and haul in slack,
Bring the rope taut, and then, with gasping breath,
Tug on through ooze and slime the sun beneath,
Which bakes and blisters—to fling back at last
A curse upon thee, when the point being past,
The sails fill, as the prow swings toward the sea.

II.

This art thou to thy namers; but to me
Thou art a faithful and a well-tried friend.
For here I watch the winds and reeds contend
In music and in dancing; while my boat
Fast by the stem, will still obedient float
To the fixed contradictions of the tides.

I often mark the flood, how it will creep
Up through the reeds, like life, or death, or sleep,
So unperceived, so stealthy, sure and still
So gently, calmly resolute of will,
As single-purposed as the man should be
Who would gain ground in living. Here I see
The harmless denizens of this lone spot
Disport themselves around, and fear me not,
Knowing I will not injure them,—my heart
Being of all wild, tameless life a part.
The marsh-wren sings her song of tenderness,
Sweet simple notes, which to the mind express
A thought of longing for the distant day
When man, the sad, heart-shackled wanderer, may
Enjoy a love untrammeled as her own.
The buzzard, luffing up, is past me blown,
Beating, close hauled, against the veering wind.
But better far than all, before, behind,
The marshes stretch, away, away, away!
A realm all limitless where Thought may stray,
Without one fear of meeting sights to bring
Pain to the heart, and check its journeying.
Where e'er we gaze an ever-spreading green,
The color of eternity, is seen
Sweeping afar, to meet at last the sky,—
Infinity linked with infinity!
Hail, wide expanse forever unreclaimed,
Which means unconquered, and for aye untamed,
Free from the seams and scars which leave the plough,
Wearing one aspect from the first till now,—
All hail, great marsh! for thou art of the sea,
With billows full as green and heart as free!

Thus art thou, "No Man's Friend," a quiet home
Where one love-mad, for Nature's sake, may come,
To watch the many-folded clouds, and see
The sky, their land, in its entirety;
To learn the calm that reigns above, below,
And kneel at Nature's feet, as I do now.

III.

The clouds sweep onward with a steady motion,
Changing their shapes and aspects as they go,
Seeking or leaving their vast home the ocean,
Taught by its currents, children of its flow.
They have the gait of Time, now fast, now slow,
Yet smooth like his; they glide away forever,
Unchecked, unjarred, unjaded by endeavor.
That is the jar which wrecks our human frames!
That effort rhythmic, yet capricious: aims
Now near and plain, now faint and far away,
While we, with starts and stops, by night and day,
Toil on in anguish, stumbling, bounding, falling,
Sinking and clinging, staggering up and calling
On Heaven for aid—yet on, forever on!
Though our torn feet be bleeding to the bone,
Our flesh and garments tatters, and our eyes
Too blinded to discern, as we arise,
The path to follow—on, forever on!
Through piercing briar and o'er cutting stone,
Through chilling wood, o'er bare sun-blistering hill,
Through icy torrent—onward, onward still!
Dying at last unconscious if we have
Gained some slight eminence to be our grave.

IV.

The foamless waves of green roll o'er the meadows,
Urged by the gusts, and whirling in their flow,
Bearing upon their swell the somber shadows
Sent from the snowy clouds,—as dark thoughts go
Forth from the minds most overcharged with light.
This home of restless winds and changing sky,
This earthly reflex of Eternity,
Which is but change, will guide the mind away
From this one spot of time where chained to-day
We pine and perish, to a pure far time
When man shall live unstained by blood and crime;
When progress steadily shall fill the sail
Which now is only flapping, and the veil
Be rent from truth, and love begin to reign,
Forging a scepter from his broken chain;
When prejudice has manumitted art,
Freeman at last, strained close to beauty's heart!
Oh, no, the love of beauty is not dead!
She sleeps—it looks like death—but have no dread,
She only sleeps.—'Tis but a little while
And she will wake, and with a beaming smile
Light all the world around her. And 'tis ours
To deck her chamber with the fairest flowers
That we can cull, and everything prepare
To greet her sight; that when, with joyful air,
She asks who planned to cheer her on the day
Of her great waking, those around may say,—
Checking all sadness as she wakes from sleep—
They rest, as thou, whilst they their watch did keep.

"NOX ERAT, ET LUNA FULGEBAT"

B. C. 218—A. D. 1800.

I.

THE foot-hills of the Alps at eventide,
The foot-hills of the Alps, ah, long ago;
Daylight and night commingling; and beside
A permeating and ethereal flow
Of moonlight, clothing all the world below
In magic mystery. Who now could tell
Shadows from shapes? On high the eternal snow
Gleams ghostly over forest, rock and fell,
Giving to solitude its most o'erpowering spell.

II.

And yet this solitude is none to-night;
Silence there is, a silence of dread sound.
Anon strange masses steal in doubtful sight;
A tramp of thousands shakes the rugged ground,
Yet muffled all as by some thought profound—
No laugh nor jest is heard, nor soldier's cry,
Even the neigh of steeds is quickly drowned—
An army toward the passes creeps on high,
Mounting with awful tread toward sleeping Italy.

III.

And as they slowly climb the rocky way,
Their leader, Afric's hope, and joy and pride,
Projects his glance of penetrating ray
From a high rock the narrow path beside,
Where he hath climbed to watch the rising tide
Of Punic power that Italy shall quell;
To see no ill their struggling march betide,
And mark if orders have been mastered well,
While thoughts of pride and power within him wildly
    swell.

IV.

But as he turns, contented, to descend,
Sudden he sees what had struck panic fear
To any heart save his; for, Heaven forefend!
Another host is seen swift gathering near,
Now dim and mingling, now distinct and clear;
Men to great engines harnessed strain and strive,
Yet stiller than his own, no whispering cheer,
Nor tramp is heard, no murmurings faint arrive,
And yet the Western steeps seem bristling, alive!

V.

Has Rome then guessed the secret of his soul,
And whelmed his flank? Look how they gather there!
The moonlight glimmers treacherous o'er the whole,
For now they disappear, and now on air
They seem to tread; anon, with withering care,
He sees them plain, their lances glisten cold;

While by a strange small man, imperious, spare,
All-masterful, their movements are controlled,
Who wears a headgear odd of a three-cornered mold.

VI.

A halt is called, from rank to rank it goes
In smothered tones, the order of command;
The legions stop, then wheel to meet their foes,
If such there be, who have this onset planned,
Guessing the secret of the master hand
That guides their course. Spies sent return and say
That nowhere can they find a hostile band,
All sleeps serene beneath the moon's cold sway,
No foe assails their flank, nor blocks their onward
     way.

VII.

The ruler of that host again ascends
His vantage rock, and through the moonlight shades
Full far and near his piercing vision bends
O'er the late bristling steeps and peopled glades—
Where are the men, their steeds and flashing blades?
Of all that throng there now remains not one,
Each fancied shape a second glance evades;
Phantoms or men, the moving forms are gone;
He and his fateful band are with the Alps alone.

VIII.

The glaciers gleam inscrutable on high;
The glaciers' breath, a thin and chilly breeze,
Sweeps from the upward pass, and absently

Plays through the gnarled and stunted sentried trees,
Which dare no farther mount. By slow degrees
All hearts are lightened of their passing gloom;
"Onward," the order comes, and backward frees
Each fetter'd rank. Their march they now resume,
Moving toward victory, or toward the awaiting tomb.

IX.

To cheer his soldiers as the omen may,
Their chief the augur summons; and concealed
Within a rocky glen beside the way,
A fire is kindled, and the fate is sealed
Of the poor victims, that may be revealed
The meaning of the portent. Flickering high
The firelight plays o'er face and lance and shield,
And tints the augur's robe, and shrouds his eye,
While he, exalted, speaks the words of destiny.

X.

"Know, leader, that the shapes which thou hast seen
Are images of things that yet shall be;
Slow-creeping centuries must intervene
Ere here shall stand another like to thee;
They presage thee a mighty victory,
And fame enduring, from that bloody strife,
So long as pride shall feed mortality
And lusts of war within man's heart be rife,
And universal death remain the law of life."

XI.

And now the word of omen "Victory"
Flies through the host; once more that muffled tread,
The creak of tightening traces, and the sigh
Of climbing thousands make a murmur dread.
The rear-guard of the pass has gained the head,
Their moonlit spears sink slowly toward the plain.
The augur's fire dies down, for aye unfed;
The passes sleep beneath the moon's calm reign,
For twenty centuries unpeopled to remain.*

* Of course, it is well known that Hannibal is supposed by certain
authorities to have crossed by way of the Little rather than the Great
St. Bernard; but the general neighborhood is the same, and Aosta is the
terminus, so to speak, of both passes.

THE BELL.

CLANG!—how it sweeps, so masterful and solemn!
So stern, so grimly definite in scope;
A battering ram of sound, one mighty column
To crush the walls of hope.

The human hands which cast and hung its tissue
Were but the tools of spirits, ruled in turn
By unimaginable lots which issue
From Nature's mystic urn.

Clang—once again! the interval how massive!
A silence as resistless as the tone;
Voicing the will of powers stern, impassive,
To us but vaguely known.

Clang—just one stroke! we may not choose but listen,
It holds, invades, commands, subdues the ear,
Making the heart to thrill, the eye to glisten,
With hope-bemantled fear.

And oh, the pitch! that restless fifth forever!
Could ye not, spirits, tune it to the chord?
There is an octave of the soul's endeavor,
We feel it, though unheard.

Nay, is there none, no prime to this wild partial
Which sweeps discordant o'er the wastes of time?
The bell clangs on, our lingering steps to marshal
Toward the unknown clime.

SONNETS.

SONNETS.

"Tristitiam et metum tradam ventis."

"Sorrow and care unto the winds I cast!"
Ay, at thy death, sad mortal, not before—
For all men their accumulated store
Of care and sorrow, when they breathe their last,
Give to the gloomy winds, grim legacy!
The winds, with steps now sluggish and now fast,
Like Christ's disciples going forth alone,
With every note of wail from sob to sigh,
From stifled moans to shrieks of agony,
Each by a different way, 'neath cloud and sun,
Go wandering o'er the world; and each doth bear
His separate load of sorrow and of care.
Their burdens sad they scatter far and near,
And sift through every cranny of the sphere.

A TIME-GLIMPSE.

One ghostly spire beneath the ghostly moon,
No cloud upon the blue yet misty sky,
The monster City sunk, as in a swoon,
In utter stillness; from a casement high
I gaze and gaze, and watch the red lights die
In distant panes, as lives go out. I see
(For time seems stopped as if to take some note
Of his long voyage) from dim futurity
Back through the past; and yet my life doth float,
Like a lost sailor in an open boat,
On one small spot of time to the dark sea:
A passion-filled, swift-thrilling human frame
Hath kindled mine,—my soul doth glow the same,—
We all are falling sparks of passion's eager flame.

HOPE.

THERE is a spring within our souls, whose rise
Is not in infancy, yet long before
The many tints of dawn in youth's clear skies
Begin to fade. At first 'tis nothing more
Than a green moisture, then a mimic shore
Encircles one bright bubble, which the rays
Of morning suns delight to dance upon.
And still, as creep away the long, long days,
Its crystal surface widens, and displays
Within its depths a nature of its own,—
Fairer than nature.—But a point of scum
Forms, thickens, spreads; and rising from beneath,
Grow ghastly weeds, and leprous patches come;
While fall the withered leaves, and choke it up with
　　death.

TO MY CORPSE.

CRUMBLE, crumble, crumble, crumble buried clay;
Crumble, crumble, crumble, flesh and bones away!
Crumble gently, slowly, 'neath the morning light,
Crumble 'neath the star-beams of the blazoned night;
Crumble while the North wind cold and cloudless
    blows,
Crumble 'neath the driving, piling, whirling snows;
Crumble while new ages spring to life and love,
Crumble in negation of the joys above—
        But the passion born of you,
        Even though unmarked, shall be
        Sifted all the wide world through,
        Over earth and air and sea,
        Ever fresh and strong and new
        In its lost identity.

THE "WINDOW" IN ORION.

As through that wondrous casement in the sky
The midnight watcher with his glass can see
The awful vistas of infinity
Stretching in dread perspective, and descry
System by system backed, and sun by sun,
While firmament out-peoples firmament
With jostling, nameless stars—so all intent
Upon some present scene, and all at one
With its too human passion, suddenly
I see new firmaments of thought appear,
But oh, so far! so far they are not clear,
Yet nebulously bright. But while the eye
Struggles toward these new worlds of the soul,
The hurrying clouds of Earth before them ever roll.

THE WORLD.

Art thou so small, oh world, thou canst not hold
A single grave without being overfilled?
Art thou so weak a single tomb can prove
Too great a burden? Are the tints so faint
Which give their colors to thy thoughts and thee
That this lone grave can lend thee all its hues?
Thy skies are tinted by forget-me-nots
Which cluster at its foot; and o'er the green
Of all thy waves and all thy living swards
Is spread a deepening melancholy hue
From its long ivy tendrils; and thy clouds
Are shaded to its granite's rigid gray.
Thy voices all its flood of silence drowns,
Thy thoughts its overflow of vacancy.

POEMS IN UMBER.

ÉMILE ZOLA.

Across the world one more *forever* booms,
The only echo from the doors of death:
Forever lost to us of sight and breath,
Forever found for those whose scattered tombs
Mark out Time's pathway. Oh, remorseless Past,
We are so poor, and thou so rich—thou hast
Them all—couldst thou no longer spare us him,
The wingless Hugo of our wingless time,
The first in clay to fashion the sublime;
The "Realist," the man whose sight, if dim
For distances, outpierced all others near,
The real heart unchilled by the world's fear;
The first to make reply to Pilate's grim
And searching question of eternal youth,
With the immortal answer, truth is truth.
Ay, truth is truth, the element which gives
Their strength to all things which 'mongst men
        endure;
Yet midst the tarnish of our earthly lives
It never can exist detached and pure.
It is the violet ray of the mind's light,
An inward impulse, not an outward sight.
Spirit, now but a fame, thy rays seem cold
Regarded through our tears, which cannot fall
For those whose bright forever has grown old
In luster and in aid that grief forestall.

Farewell, farewell, all hast thou now but life,
And we naught save the instinct of the strife.
The lamps of earth, alas, are faint and few,
Warmth need we here our courage to renew,
The heaven of art is high and oh, so far!
We pine to see thy lamp rekindled as a star.

DESPONDENCY.

Woods of the spirit land,
Your leaflets touch and pluck me as I go,
Your branches beckoning on every hand
Wave to and fro—
Woods nipped and sere
All cold and drear,
A fading light and falling night,
Where shall I go?
Winds of the spirit waste,
The while my feet grow heavy as I tread,
Ye seem with voices, trembling with chill haste,
To call the dead.
Calling me to them, calling them to me,
And leaving us confronted as ye flee
Away, away, with distant whisperings dread.
Fallen is the night,
Perished the light,
Is there no track nor trail which leads from here?
Despair low whispers, it will ne'er appear;
For in a magic circle dost thou wander,
And aye in vain thy failing forces squander,
And though a light will shine upon thee soon,
'Twill only be the spectral, shadow-peopling moon.

A MIDNIGHT COLLOQUY.

His Soul.
OH, how the night lowers dark!
Oh, whither this down-tending way?
I dare follow no farther—oh, hark
To my prayers, tell me, where leads the way?

He.
Love me, only love me still
Keep my hand,
Nearer stand.
Over many a sunny hill,
In the happy days, hast thou
Followed as the waters flow,
Careless, trusting, without will—
Cheer me now!

His Soul.
The darkness swims round me, I fall!
'Tis my death to have trusted in vain—
How *couldst* thou? I came at thy call,
I heard thee with joy that was pain,
So potent thy speech to enthral;

And I followed, still followed.—What! all,
All false, all thy promises sweet
Which checked my instinctive retreat?
All true, all the doubts of thy skill,

Of thy honor? I followed thee still,
Though the joys of the way did expire,
Though I saw thee abusing my will,
Leading downward through darkness and mire—
And now?

He.

And now?

Both.

Turn back, turn back, retrace our way,
Or find some path which leads to day,
To purity and peace and love,
Which shine above.
Tell us, Earth, is there no way,
However difficult, to-day?
For sunken hearts which upward yearn
Is there, is there no return?

Echo.

No return.

NOVEMBER.

LEAFLESS and dry and still! How weak the shadows,
How pale the sun far down the Southern sky,
How russet are the woods, how buff the meadows—
Tints everywhere of cold and neutral dye!

The ineffectual sunbeams feebly glancing
From trunk to trunk amidst the forest trees;
The bangles of the sycamore are dancing
To the thin, chilly breeze.

What contrast, as on high they dance fantastic,
Lightfooted, eerie, frivolous and gay,
To the reserve, reëntrant and monastic,
Which wraps this landscape gray.

I love this solitude—may none invade it—
The only love I know;
My heart is what the world has slowly made it—
A scene expecting snow.

A HYMN OF PAIN.

SEE how the rain of human tears is falling
In blinding gusts which dim Earth's every shore,
And woe to woe and sob to sob is calling,
Unheard, unanswered in the tempest's roar.

The rain of human tears, which ever beating,
Beats down and levels, with its steady shower,
New-sodded graves, so thick their sides are meeting,
That fade from sight each day and every hour.

Yet still they rise! their grasses interweaving,
Until they form one widespread mound of pain,
The swelling sigh of Earth's torn bosom heaving,
Forever sinking but to rise again.

Oh, blessed day when all redeemed from anguish,
When, like the moon, all airless and serene,
The World, with none to die and none to languish,
Shall roll through space with pure and silver sheen.

When to her heart at last the boon is given
To pass the time to man and grief allowed,
And to resume her place, a queen in heaven,
Her glories wrapt no more in sorrow's cloud.

THE SHORELESS SEA.

A SEALESS shore wakes no alarm,
Then why a shoreless sea?
From you none ever suffered harm,
Waves of Eternity.

Friends of the past, the rocks of time
Behind, beside, before,
Around me stretch, a stormy clime
Awakes the billows' roar.

But ye afar are safe, serene,
While here we toss and strain;
Ye saw the treach'rous breakers' sheen,
And sought the open main.

The moon is up, the night is near,
The ruddy sunset, dimly clear,
Still tips your distant sails.
Oh, may I, ere this faint light fails,
Lay close the course which you did steer—
Naught else on earth avails.

IN MEMORY OF JOHN WISTER, OF VERNON.

Born 1804. Died Jan. 28th, 1883.

SLOW came the morning, slow, with features pale,
White-robed, close-muffled in a misty veil.
She seemed to feel that Death was at her side,
And thus like him all stealthily to glide,
And emulate his footfall and his hue.
She came; but yet unmarked of one who knew
Fair Nature in her subtlest changing mood,
Beloved companion of his solitude,
Who could predict the aspects of her face,
For whom her smiles and frowns had equal grace.
She came unmarked—he slept, and slept for aye.
What lesser sleep than an eternity
Could balance that unrest beyond control,
That life-long, inner combat of a soul
Framed for the whirlwind, yet becalmed through life?
Cast in mad times of tumult and of strife,
Of popular uprising and of rage,
Strong in the storm within him, to assuage
The tempest, and to rule a surging sea
Of uncouth men had been his destiny.
His mighty strength, his ready eloquence,
His light and feathery fancy, solid sense,
His tender heart (to him was childhood dear),
His courage never tarnished by a fear,

In other times and scenes had made his name
Known of his kind, perchance of lasting fame.
But now obscure, as glad of rest, he sleeps,
And one who loved him well in silence weeps.
Up to the dizzy verge of death we climb,
And peer into the dark abysm of time
Which has engulfed this strong Reality—
Then sighing, journey on, and pondering, sigh.

THE VERNON CLOCK.

Tick, tock, tick, tock, a strange and solemn sound!
Tick, tock, tick, tock, a tone akin to things beneath
    the ground.
To things beneath the ground about to be,
To things beneath the ground which are no more,—
A murmur of the all-engulfing sea,
Which still grows clearer as we near the shore.

Tick, tock, tick, tock, the pendulum swings heavily
    and slow,
The rustle of Time's garments, and the chime
Is but his footfall; as the quarters go,
They speak the quarters of our lives with power,
And hint of him who comes to strike the hour.
Even as a merchant counts us out our gold,
Which we are free to spend in good or ill,
So the old clock, with neutral mien and cold,
Counts us the moments we may waste at will.

Kind friends, I cannot waste them as of yore,
The flush and fire and haste have passed away.
Ye took my gladness when ye went before,—
Could you not leave it for my little day?
Nor can I freely spend them all alone;
I can but sit, as nears the mid of night,
And question the old clock of hours flown,
And ask of scenes that passed beneath his sight.

Kind friends, the clock beheld you one and all—
First those of old, and then us gathered there—
Within your beautiful and stately hall,
And still ticks on, while you are less than air.
It saw the rush and revelry and glare,
And hurrying feet,
And eyes that meet,
And lips that long to kiss, half shy, half bold.
Inscrutable,
Immutable,
Slow ringing,
Still swinging,
It ticked each hush as ye lay lifeless there;
It saw us bend o'er the last forehead cold,
Then saw the walls stripped, tenantless and bare.

Tick, tock, tick, tock, a strange and solemn tone!
An echo of the voices of the blest,
A sound which bears me on to those at rest,
Who for an hour have left me here alone;
A sound both grim and grand, both stern and free,—
The whisper of the shell to time's eternal sea.

J. F. H.

Obiit 1878.

"Pauline, image de ma belle vie!"
—*Balzac.*

O HEART too early waning,
Rough Grief's too tender prey!
Thy power to feel
But urged the steel
Of Pain thy peace to slay.

Yet some through life are gaining
A tolerance of woe,
The power to bear
Increase of care
With every ill doth grow;

And some, like wild dogs speeding,
Across life's broken waste,
O'er hill and dale
Have kept the trail
Which the phantom fame hath traced.

Their bleeding feet unheeding,
These blindly follow swift,
And one by one
Sink down alone
In secret glade and rift.

But what of thee, bright creature
Created but in vain,
Wert thou but made
To cast a shade
Like rocks upon a plain?

Was all that from each feature
Flashed forth, the love, the pride,
Formed for an hour,
A sport of power,
A boast and naught beside?

My eyes are ever seeing
Thy golden tresses fair,
Thy dark eyes' fire—
Love, hope, desire—
Through mists of chill despair.

O, mystery of being,
That meeting which decreed
That one in pain
Should turn again,
And one in pain proceed.

THE SOUL'S BANQUET.

Oh yes, it was a lovely night—
The moon was at the full, and near
The summit of her steady flight;
My heart was young, my heart was light,
My heart was pure and clear.
My feast was ready, and I called them all,
From east and west, to come and share with me,
I deemed it good and beautiful; my call
I thought would bring a surging sea
Of guests to jostle and to feast.
My summons ceased.
The silence had increased.
No, not one footfall could I hear
To prove my voice had reached one living thing.
The silence round me changed from grand to drear,
From drear it grew to menacing.

But I was young, and so with hope imbued,
With all my skill I still my feast renewed,
And still I called; but still they did not come.
Perchance I thought I called, and was but dumb.
Days came and went, yet all the same:
The board stood loaded, all alone,
The flowers bloomed, the crystals shone—
No merry-makers came.
At last, upon the horizon's rim
I saw a speck, 'twas faint and dim;

But nearing fast, it grew and grew
Until a living shape I knew.
Then others joined, in threes and fours—
They came, a group, a squad, a crowd,
Toward the board a column pours—
They are my guests at last arriving.
They are my guests, but all in black,
And wrangling, too, with voices loud.
They wait no signal of attack,
At everything, each, all are driving.
They have the flowers quite destroyed,
The viands they have all devoured,
The vases broken, and have showered
The wines upon the sward. Uncloyed,
Unsated, on a sudden they arise,
And hasten from their havoc with hoarse, rasping
    cries.

Fools only deem their case is rare,
That theirs are consecrated woes;
And yet it makes the form more spare,
The while the eye more furtive grows,
To think that what we did prepare,
And spread with so much pride and care,
Was only food for crows.

ACQUIESCENCE.

Oh, what the Power with life inwove
Which makes us but to mar?
Which plants and tends and garners love
To scatter it afar.

Which makes the tendrils of the heart
To man and beast and tree
Cling as if never more to part,
Only to tear them free.

Which casts the joy-bell of the mind,
But tunes it to a knell;
And makes *forever* ever find
Its echo in *farewell*.

"Forever *there*," a poet sings—
But where? Through depths profound,
From cliff to cliff the echo rings,
A cold abysmal sound.

Whoever has the close-tuned ear
To catch the undertone,
In every song a dirge can hear,
In every laugh a groan.

'Tis man who has his world outgrown,
His hopes, thoughts, wishes fly
Beyond his atmospheric zone,
To tumble from the sky;

To fall to Earth, who gathers all,
And, on her endless way,
Smiles gently o'er the throes that gall
Her animated clay.

THE FARTHER SHORE.

Away, away, my gaze is far away,
Through many a cold and perished night and day,
Which float transparent, like the layers that lie
Upon the confines of an Autumn sky,
In dim aerial distances. I gaze
Backward, still backward through the farthest haze,
And our dim tracks across the world I see
Since first we journeyed on in company.
My eye can follow on o'er crag and glen,
O'er prairies and through forest, copse and fen,
Beginning where my footprints first are shown
Small, slipping, faintly pressed beside thine own,
Then on to where they grow more firm than thine,
On to a strand where now are only mine—
That surfless coast bereft of ocean's roar,
Where the wind ever blows from off the shore.
Where, at the utmost limit of the way
Which we might tread together, in the gray
And spectral light of an Autumnal morn,
I stood and saw thee o'er the waters borne
Far from the world I know of joy and pain,
Beyond my utmost vision's utmost strain.
I live upon the sands of that grim sea,
And by the ripple of Eternity
My ears are ever filled; and fast or slow,
I pace the shore forever to and fro,
Walking through ghosts which need not step aside

To give me way. Beside the somber tide
'Tis thus my fate to wander, and to peer,
Through the transparent figures clustered near,
Far o'er the distant reaches of the sea;
Watching, with an unbidden constancy,
That outline dim which drifts the winds before,
That land-like cloud they call the farther shore.

LINES IN MY MOTHER'S MEMORY.

I.

Mother, no Spring was e'er so beautiful,
So vainly beautiful, so over-fair,
With joy so radiant and of health so full
As this, for me the first thou canst not share.
All Winter long I roamed each corridor,
The empty hall, the desolate chambers wide
(Except one room, untrod forevermore),
And saw with furtive half-averted looks,
The paintings, tapestries, plates, carvings, books,
All blank, expectant, idle, misapplied—
Absent they echoed back, and naught beside,
Yet absent only from one little place.
Now Spring has called me forth to gaze in space,
In act or thought to roam o'er earth and sea,
And view each scene where thou hast been, couldst
    be—
Wide as the prospect, still thou wert not there—
I 'gin to feel thou art not anywhere.

II.

The flowers thou hast planted long delayed
Their coming, as in doubt and half dismayed,
Fearing to find thee not; and now they stand
And only seem a lesson to repeat,

And wave unmeaningly,
Wanting thy tender hand,
Lost in the land,
As lost as I.
In vain they strive my lostness to beguile—
Yes, with a sweet, but oh, so vacant smile!

III.

I dread the porch, the altered scene
Of many a pleasant evening talk.
In every winding garden-walk,—
Where all thy mite of joy hath been,—
I seem to hear thy feeble feet.
At every turn I look to meet
That stately form, half stooping now,
Yet nobly bent, as grief but bends,
Chastened and dignified by woe,
With that sad grace of vanquished pride
Which sorrow gives to make amends
For having taken all beside.

IV.

Ere driven by unrest's necessity,
I painfully displace and scatter far
The things which thou didst prize, or ere again,
Pursuing still my ever-clouded star,
I troubled sail the troubled sea,
Instinctive still, I look farewell
Where most thy absence now doth dwell,
That echo of thy presence vain.

The favorite seat deserted now;
The vacant pane where, from below,
I met thy sad, fond welcome here;
The expected step ne'er heard to fall,
Yet ever sounding in the ear;
The labeled work, the folded shawl,
The cherished book whose corners curled
Are dim with dust; the garnished bed
Which desolate yawns untenanted;
The empty room, the house, the world,
Reëcho, *lost forevermore!*
I give one last, long, wistful gaze
Of restless sorrow and amaze,
And all unhomed, push off from shore.

V.

Sea, sea and sky, and many a wind!
We long have left the shore,—
The horizon closing in behind,
And gliding on before.
Lovers of shallows, waters emerald green,
How swift ye fade! and ever deepening blue,
Supplanting you, on every side is seen,—
Seas wilder, freer, native waves, than you.
For other minds they bear a mystic charm,
These wild waves which the wild winds urge,
Hearts bound with joy, half mingled with alarm,
Catching the freedom of the surge.
To me they paint the troubled soul,
As types, and naught beside,
Emblems of an immense regret

As desolate, deep and wide.
Swell onward, billows, foam and fret,
Though fast and far ye roll,
My sorrow's sight beyond you yet
Can pierce without control.
Beyond your farthest Western line,
Where shifting clouds and foam combine
I ever see one sacred spot
Upon a hillside lone,
Where blooms and fades forget-me-not
Beside an ivied stone.

VI.

It is not mist which fills the Rhone's wide vale,
But air made visible; a purple hue,
Living and flushed, hangs o'er each pointed sail
That dreams o'er Leman's waters; tiers of blue
Rise, ever fainter tinted, toward the sky—
Pierced by the sun with planes of mystery—
To merge beneath the highest mountain peaks
In a thin pearl, through which in serried streaks
The glaciers shine—a chilly light and stern,
Born to repel, yet cause the heart to yearn,—
Serene, reserved, contained, yet strangely clear,—
A light as of some dawn, but not of this, our Sphere.
The Dent du Midi's seven castled peaks,
From their aërial sea,
Rear high in space their wind-cut, snowy towers,
And lift my heart aloft to Heaven and *thee.*
My thoughts go backward to that awful morning,
Nor night nor dawn, when by some freak of Time,
I stood with thee upon a wilder summit,

A pass e'en more sublime.
To when, with ice and snow above, around me,—
The mind's eternal snow,—
I stood upon that cloud-enveloped frontier
Which lies betwixt the lands of peace and woe.
I felt a deadly numbness creeping o'er me,
Heard the faint words, "Forget me not, my son,"
Then rallying quick, I bid thee be of courage—
And found myself alone.
Slow I descended, slow, with backward glances
And many sighs and tears,
Leaving that valley which for me forever
Henceforth had fewer fears.
From out the shadows circling close around me
Upon my heart there fell
A shade no joy of life shall wholly scatter,—
Not even music's spell;
To stay till merged in universal shadow,
It shall with night entwine,
When next I stand upon that icy summit,
Prepared to pass the line.

VII.

Farewell, pure heart, that through life's darksome
    region,
Where noxious vapors eddy through the night,
And staining shadows menace by the legion,
Passed with unaltered light.
Red is my torch,—its flickering earthly glimmer,
Flaring and falling, through the mirk is shown;
Yet if at times there gleams a purer shimmer,
That ray is all thine own.

VIII.

Forgive me if without thy smile,
With none to know or care,
I struggle here a little while—
Not born to feed despair.
It is thy spirit keeps me still
In the world's lists, thy dauntless will
(Oh, would that more of thee were mine!)
Which could not flinch, and would not pine.
Blown, jostled, stricken, bowed with pain,
Borne backward in the contest vain,
Stubborn I strive, and wait the day
When I, at last, may sigh and say,
"The fight is ended, lost or won—
I did not yield, and yet 'tis done."

IX.

Farewell, farewell, I cannot hope
To reach thy soul's far higher scope,
Yet in my life, while lingering here,
May still some trace of thee appear.
Oh, may I more deserve thy pride,
Oh, may that power to curb and guide,
Oft foiled by my wild, wayward will,
Forever more with me abide,
And check my passions' surging tide—
Now that thy voice, heard but by me,
Amidst the mountains, by the sea—
Ne'er silent when I am alone—
Has gained that awesome, tender tone
Of realms so calm and still.